Triumvirate

THREE PLAYS

by

Peter Carlaftes

THREE ROOMS PRESS

NEW YORK CITY

For the life in the days of a theater.

Cover and Interior Design:
Kat Georges Design, New York, NY
katgeorges.com

First Edition

Printed in the United States of America

ISBN: 978-0-9840700-6-0

Printed in the United States of America
Text set in ITC New Baskerville.

Published by Three Rooms Press | New York, NY
www.threeroomspress.com
email: info@threeroomspress.com

INTRODUCTION

For most of the last decade of the Twentieth Century, the Marilyn Monroe Memorial Theater inhabited the space at 96 Lafayette Street in San Francisco. Call it what you will: A storefront theater, a blackbox theater, a stage. One thing for sure—it was a cauldron of creative energy. A place to experiment, try new ideas, develop craft. From 1992 through 2000, Peter Carlaftes and I staged 22 original plays, in addition to numerous adaptations and deconstructions of classic theater, dozens of improv nights, independent movie nights, "new look" nights, poetry readings, creative "happenings" and more. It was magic. What remains are memories—and the writing.

Carlaftes' writing confirms he is one of the most original voices in modern theater, on both the stage and the page. His fresh vision and ability to create both heart-wrenching tragedy and side-splitting comedy (often within the same piece) marks him as unique among contemporary playwrights. This book offers three sensational plays from the body of work he developed at The Marilyn. Reading them is a pure delight that reinforces the desire to see them staged again. Enjoy.

—*Kat Georges*

CONTENTS

Spin-Dry

An
Intervention
with Sara Kinetic*

*Her mom died at Altamont. Her dad in Outer Space.

PRODUCTION NOTES:

A few years after its initial run, we performed *Spin-Dry* at The Marilyn once as a special event on New Year's Eve. That night, after the piece (which ran on all cylinders), the audience was profoundly disconnected from pursuing the celebratory norm. That is success as far as theater is concerned. With its barrage of sound, slides and TV snow, coupled with the non-redeeming qualities endearing every character, *Spin-Dry* broke through the fortress of expectations and enabled audience members to look at themselves with fresh new eyes, undistilled by manipulative marketing that the modern world thrusts upon its inhabitants.

The tagline for *Spin-Dry* is what opened the door to its creation: The character of Sara Kinetic, through certain twists of fate, was raised by her stepmother and stepfather, who married after her real parents died by iconically American means. Read on.

—*P.C.*

SPIN DRY

SETTING:

Smack Dab Mid-Nineties inside Second Wind, a Detox Retreat for the Stars.

CHARACTERS:

SARA KINETIC: *33-year-old talk show host in third week of stress-hiatus; first time patient at Second Wind.*

DR. AMELIA RATE: *Second Wind's intuitive 34-year-old clinical program director.*

LILY GABLES-SWEENY: *60-year-old widow and divorcée, at Second Wind for the first time to visit her stepdaughter, Sara.*

JIMMY SHELTER: *26-year-old rock star; frontman of the Ex-Laws; frequent patient at Second Wind.*

GUY LIMBO: *29-year-old action movie star; newly arrived at Second Wind to prepare for his role as replacement ballplayer, Glen Scott Toby (nickname "Costco"), in the upcoming drama flick, "Full Count."*

DR. FREDDIE DEVILLE: *Second Wind's 40-year-old guru/prime mover.*

PROLOGUE:
Setting the Stage

Pre-show Audio: Sixties Muzak fills the theatre. Dim stagelights expose the activity room SL.

Setting:

SL: ACTIVITY ROOM: *A Seventies couch, set at an angle. Above it,* DS, *a monitor hangs from the ceiling, facing the audience. Behind couch, a large indoor palm tree. One chair at the* US *end of couch, facing out.*

UCS: OFFICE: *A desk with two chairs.*

SR: BEDROOM: *A bed, angled out, with a small chair. On* USR *wall, space for posters used to indicate whose room we are in.*

Audio: Fade music to silence. Lights fade to black.

VOICEOVER: This is for _____ *(Name of any celebrity currently in rehab).*

CAST: *(Offstage)* Who?

Audio: Instrumental version of "Cast Your Fate to the Wind" begins, mixed with a sporadic medley of self-help quips recorded from daytime television.

A slide appears on USC *wall that reads "TUESDAY."*

SCENE I:
Sara's Room; 1:30 p.m.

Audio fades. Slide off.

SARA, *in her room, sits on her bed in the lotus position. On back wall is poster of a happy face with a frown.* DR. RATE *and* LILY *approach from off-stage in mid-conversation.*

LILY: I turned on my TV in Rio de Janeiro and there she was . . . My Sara in Spanish.

DR. RATE: We have her on Prequil an anti-depressant . . . Delete negativity—Insert focus.

LILY: The TV set wasn't really mine . . . It belonged to the hotel. Ever been to Rio?

DR. RATE: Her room's bright and airy, Mrs Gables-Sweeny.

LILY: Please call me Lily.

DR. RATE: Southeastern exposure.

LILY: Sara, you see well, isn't my daughter . . . I married her father.

DR. RATE: She told me you taught her to play the piano.

LILY: To believe looking back—I was beautiful once.

DR. RATE: She's in the next room.

LILY: God, I'm excited!

DR. RATE: I'll tell her you're here.

LILY: It's been so long.

DR. RATE *knocks Beethoven's Fifth on* SARA'S *door.*

DR. RATE: Sara?

SARA: Yes, Doctor?

DR. RATE: May I come in?

SARA: Fan mail from some flounder?

DR. RATE: There's someone to see you.

SARA: Who?

LILY: Surprise, Hon-Bun!

SARA *screams.*

Lights up sharp.

LILY *hugs* SARA *after the scream.* DR. RATE *stands by the entry.*

SARA: Sara Kinetic . . . This is your life.

LILY: Look at her, Why—She's the picture of health.

JIMMY SHELTER *enters with a CD player blasting the Ex-Laws' new hit song. He carries a cellular phone in a shoulder holster and a harmonica in his back pocket.* DR. RATE *seems uneasy, but goes with the flow.*

JIMMY: Hey, Kinetic—Listen!

SARA: Mom . . .

JIMMY: *(Sees* LILY.*)* Wow! Live.

SARA: Meet Jimmy Shelter.

DR. RATE *glares at* JIMMY. JIMMY *turns off CD.*

LILY: Is that a gun?

JIMMY: No way, Little Sister!

SARA: It's a cell phone, Mom.

JIMMY: See—state of the art.

LILY: I've been in Europe.

SARA: Lily loves to travel.

DR. RATE: Well I'm sure that Sara would like to spend some time alone with her mother.

JIMMY: Say no more, Doc. *(To* SARA.*)* Slide by later and listen to my tunes.

LILY: Are you a musician?

JIMMY: In the flesh!

SARA: He has one of the top bands in the country.

JIMMY: Whattaya mean "one of"?

LILY: Does he play the piano?

SARA: Doctor?

DR. RATE: Yes, Sara.

SARA: This isn't working.

LILY: I was her teacher.

DR. RATE: Jimmy—

JIMMY: Yeah, Doc.

DR. RATE: Why don't you show Lily the activity room?

LILY: I'd like to watch the TV now.

JIMMY: Come on, Little Sister. What day is it?

LILY: Tuesday.

JIMMY *leads* LILY *out of the room.*

JIMMY: *(Sings.)* Goodbye—Lily Tuesday . . . Who Can . . .

LILY: *(Offstage.)* Is that a real song?

SARA: Doctor?

DR. RATE: Yes, Sara?

SARA: You gave me your word that I wouldn't recover.

Blackout.

Audio: Rolling Stones' "Ruby Tuesday."

Remove poster.

SCENE II:
Activity Room; 20 Minutes Later

Music fades. LILY *sits on the couch looking up at TV.*

TV ANNOUNCER: Good news for you unhappy campers in the Pacific Northwest . . . Sun today—but look out tomorrow. There's a cold front moving in . . . and with that low pressure system pushing up from the south—Expect the rain back by mid-Wednesday . . .

LILY: Those poor people . . .

Lights up. Snow appears on monitor whenever it's on.

DR. RATE *stands in the doorway observing* LILY.

LILY *takes breath spray from her purse, has a spritz and puts it back.*

TV ANNOUNCER: Can you believe it, Folks . . . Heavy snow across Montana and the Dakotas . . . Here it is May and there are still icicles hanging off Mount Rushmore. Teddy Roosevelt looks like FuManChu. By the time the snow melts in Big Sky Country, they'll be digging in for the coming winter.

LILY: I've never been to Montana.

LILY *takes out the same container, sprays some on her wrist, puts it away and rubs her wrist on the back of her neck.*

LILY: I think Sweeny went there in the sixties to live with wolves . . .

LILY *clicks off the TV.*

LILY: Maybe next year.

DR. RATE *enters room.*

LILY: How is she, Doctor? Is it my fault?

DR. RATE: There's nothing wrong.

LILY: Call me Lily.

DR. RATE: There's nothing wrong, Lily.

LILY: Good.

Pause. DR. RATE *sits.*

DR. RATE: Lily?

LILY: Yes, Doctor.

DR. RATE: Do you have any plans?

LILY: Well, I soon might visit Montana.

DR. RATE: How'd you like to move in with us, Lily?

LILY: What's the weather like?

DR. RATE: You see . . . Sara needs you. And I've developed a program for in-house co-dependence. *(Pause.)*

LILY: That's nice.

DR. RATE: You'd stay with Sara. You'd be her support group.

LILY: What time is it?

DR. RATE: Ten past two.

LILY: Majestic Bargains is on.

DR. RATE: Think about it, Lily.

LILY: I bought a lovely Chagall from them once.

DR. RATE: Take your time . . .

LILY: *(Reaching for the remote.)* Thank you, Doctor.

DR. RATE *exits. TV comes on.*

LILY: *(Changing channels.)* Here it is!

SARA *appears at entry; peeks into room.*

New voice on TV.

TV ANNOUNCER: What treasures await the elegant ladies and refined gentlemen in this half hour of Majestic Bargains? Okay, Who now—Who would like a Louis the XIV headrest in their automobile? That's right—Louis the XIV! Fits any car beginining with the letter "A" like . . . "A" Ford! . . . "A" Chevy . . . Or even . . . "A" Maserati!!!!

Fade audio of TV. SARA *enters room.*

SARA: Hi, Lily . . .

LILY: *(Opens her arms.)* Hon-Bun!

SARA: *(Like Father Karras's mother in The Exorcist.)* Please, Dimi . . . Why you call me that?

LILY: You are so talented.

LILY *turns her head the opposite way as* SARA *approaches.* SARA *kisses* LILY *on the side of her forehead.*

SARA: Neither one of us can feel anything.

SARA *sits in the chair farthest from* LILY.

SARA: Keeping busy?

LILY: I went to Greece last month. Did you get the sponge?

SARA: How long has it been?

LILY: God—Let me see . . .

SARA: Try seven years.

LILY: Oh that's right—I watched you on tape at the studio.

SARA: Rock Video Television: RVTV.

LILY: You had all those people jumping around for you.

SARA: That was a rock group, Lily. It was part of their act.

LILY: I saw your picture in *The Spectacle.*

SARA: Joan of Archives. Rare Rock Footage with Sara Kinetic.

LILY: The magazine said you were here.

SARA: Hey, Lily . . . Do you still carry one of those rubber dividers around with you in the supermarket?

LILY: I just don't want to feel . . . I like to have one handy. Some people don't even use them.

SARA: That's pathetic.

LILY: It's a sign of the times, Hon-Bun.

SARA: My ratings fell three points.

Pause.

LILY: Did you know that your father was a man?

SARA: You don't say!

LILY: What I meant was he was quite a man.

SARA: Carl Gables—Dead Astronaut.

LILY: You wouldn't believe how many letters I still get to this day from kids in school doing science projects . . . and veterans—mostly Vietnam veterans, going on about what a hero he was. *(Pause.)* It seems like I'm never at home.

SARA: Where is your home?

LILY: Well . . . it might be here with you.

SARA: What did you say?

LILY: Well, the Doctor explained—

SARA: Who? Dr. Rate?

LILY: Yes . . .

SARA: God that makes sense.

LILY: And—

SARA: And you want to do it?

Pause.

LILY: What do you think?

SARA: Turn on 15—

LILY: What?

SARA: Channel 15.

LILY *hands* SARA *the remote.* SARA *changes the channel.*

SARA: It's Tuesday, right? Hah! Deja Vu.

LILY: Pardon?

SARA: Nothing, Lily. A rerun.

LILY: What show is this?

SARA: My show—Me. Sara Kinetic. The theme for today is "Women Who Abuse Themselves." I found some good people. One of them actually falls down the stairs to prove a point.

Show begins. LILY *and* SARA *watch.*

TV ANNOUNCER: Welcome to The Sara Kinetic Show . . .

LILY: There she is! My little Sara.

SARA: Quiet on the set!

TV SARA KINETIC: I'm Sara Kinetic. Today's Hot Topic: "Women Who Abuse Themselves." First, we have Ann Tigoni of Fayetteville, NC—

TV ANN'S VOICE: Every time I get my period, I experience the same empty feeling . . .

LILY: *(Over TV.)* Guess what, Hun-Bun? Funny, though—I never had a period once in my life.

SARA'S *mind clicks: "What a great theme for my show!"*

Blackout. LILY *and* SARA *exit. Audio continues.*

TV SARA KINETIC: And from Wawkeegan, Illinois: Ms. Terry Cloth . . .

TV TERRY'S VOICE: See these scars? I did this. Not some man. I did it. I threw myself down the stairs. I didn't tell my friends and family that I fell because some man beat me up. I threw myself down the stairs. And you saw me. So there.

TV ANNOUNCER: And now a word from our sponsor.

SCENE III, PART 1:
Main Office

During blackout, while audio is playing, DR. DEVILLE *and* GUY LIMBO *enter.* DR. DEVILLE *sits at his desk with a houseplant in his lap (which he occasionally caresses, like a pet), processing the admittance forms for movie star* GUY LIMBO. LIMBO *sits across the desk from the doc.*

Lights up (after TV ANNOUNCER'S *last line).*

LIMBO: So the pitching coach gets me hooked snorting cocaine and my world starts slipping away. Then they settle the strike and I'm out of a job but I get a check for 20 Thousand Dollars—more money than I ever would've seen in my life!

DR. DEVILLE: Fine, fine . . . Sounds like a winner, Guy.

LIMBO: We're going with the title, "Full Count."

DR. DEVILLE: Very catchy. *(To houseplant.)* How's my little baby?

LIMBO: It's all about opression, Doc. Really packs a wallop.

DR. DEVILLE: Fine, fine . . . Who do you play?

LIMBO: Glen Scott Toby, but the guys call me "Costco."

DR. DEVILLE: Okay, Costco. Do you have any preference of rooms?

LIMBO: What the hell, Doc—you know—just the regular. And get this: The team I'm playing for, The Albuquerque Aztecs—They're an expansion team. Now this is deep. I'm a replacement for a team that never had any real players.

DR. DEVILLE: We'll put you in the Gold Medal Suite. Would you like to experience our "Dali Lava"?

LIMBO: Well, Doc . . . No. Not this time.

DR. DEVILLE: Fair enough, Costco. Here's your key. And, sign this. There, at the bottom, please. Good. *(Opens file. Hands* LIMBO *a cocaine vial.)* And you'll need this.

LIMBO: Yes!

DR. DEVILLE: To tide you over.

LIMBO *snorts cocaine.*

DR. DEVILLE: Any questions?

LIMBO: None that I can think of, Doc.

DR. DEVILLE: Fine, fine . . . I'm here if you want. *(Presses desk intercom.)* Della—Have Arthur show Costco his room.

Blackout. Phone machine beeps. LIMBO *exits.*

SCENE III, PART 2:
Main Office, Minutes Later

Message begins in blackout. Computer screen on desk.

MACHINE: Thank you for calling the Second Wind Hotline. Please hold at present. Operators are busy helping others . . .

Lights up. DR. RATE *enters and sits at the computer. watches the monitor.*

MACHINE: To make reservations . . . Press 1 now . . . *(Beep.)*

Lights on.

DR. RATE: *(Over machine voice. Punches in the numbers.)* Okay . . . 552-3034 . . .

MACHINE: If you'd like to book space for the month of June . . . Press 1 now . . . *(No beep.)*

DR. DEVILLE: Who we got?

DR. RATE: Warren Turcotte . . . 5120 Thornill Road . . .

DR. DEVILLE: Where is that?

DR RATE: Lakefield . . . Investment banker . . .

MACHINE: If you'd like to book space for the month of July . . . Press 2 now. *(Beep.)*

DR. DEVILLE: Property holdings?

DR. RATE: Nothing to speak of.

DR. DEVILLE: Fuck him. *(Presses button.)*

MACHINE: Sorry, but we are booked solid through mid-September. Please try again later and we'll —

(Click. Audio stops.)

DR. DEVILLE: So you think the Gables-Sweeny woman's really going to bite?

DR. RATE: I know it, Freddie. Lily feels needed. All you have to do is sign her up.

DR. DEVILLE: Fine, fine . . . Exceptional work.

DR. RATE: A jaded revival of the family unit.

DR. DEVILLE: Not to mention—the lady's loaded.

DR. RATE: Lily's reached the point in life where there is no point. Get my drift? She's completely disconnected.

Pause.

DR. RATE: You know the stepdaughter—Sara—could be a problem . . .

DR. DEVILLE: What's your suggestion?

DR. RATE: Upgrade her Prequil.

DR. DEVILLE: Okay, Amelia. Fine, fine . . . Starting tomorrow 8 grains a day.

DR. RATE: *(Picks up folder.)* And, who have we here?

DR. DEVILLE: New arrival.

DR. RATE: Glen Scott Toby. Nickname: Costco. Come on, DeVille— Is this a joke?

DR. DEVILLE: No joke, Rate. Six week treatment. Cash up front. *(Pause.)* There's more to him than meets the eye.

DR. RATE: Come to think of it, the guy looks familiar.

DR. DEVILLE: I'll bet you've seen his face before at least a hundred times. So, what was this about next week? You need some time off?

DR. RATE: I'm doing a seminar in San Clemente.

DR. DEVILLE: Fine, fine . . . Oh, wait. Here—I almost forgot. This agent called for you around 1 o'clock. Something about a studio audition. *(Pets and coos to houseplant.)* How's my little baby?

DR. RATE: So, Freddie?

DR. DEVILLE: Yes?

DR. RATE: We still on for dinner?

DR. DEVILLE: Why, certainly, Amelia. . . *(Short pause.)* I'll tell you the story of Costco . . .

Blackout.

Audio: Rock music begins.

Exit DR. RATE *and* DR. DEVILLE.

Enter JIMMY.

SCENE IV:
Jimmy's Room; 3:45 p.m.

Music continues until JIMMY *turns it off. Lights on on* JIMMY'S *room. Poster on wall reads "Suppose They Gave a Concert and Nobody Came?"*

JIMMY: *(Talking on cell phone.)* Bullshit, Baby . . . Loud and clear coming through. Look out . . . Get this, you handful of nothing—. . . Good. Fuck all the burnouts from W-2. Don't try that shit with me. I got no conscience . . . Fuck Paolo, Fuck Ritchie and Steeltoe, too. That's how it is. I wrote the songs— . . . I don't give a dry shit if Paolo needs money so the baby can have a bone transplant. The buck stops here, Pal. It's my music—. . . Well they ain't gonna get dollar one outta me—. . . Sue the fucking label. Hire Hiawatha. My heart's with you, Brother. Goodbye and good luck. *(Hangs up.)*

So I'm Jimmy Shelter and I'll ream out the planet. Give a little whistle. Who's next? *(Puts phone in holster.)* You can't whistle worth a shit with a mouth full of crackers. Wasn't age of three profound?

(Takes out vial of Liquid Methedrine mixed with Echinacea and unscrews the cap.) Blue Hawaii . . . See me coming . . . Off the deep end. You won't see me. *(Squirts methedrine drops into his mouth. Turns off music.)*

Why I just got to thinking of my old pal, Stack. Ladies man. Fancy dresser. Owned seven jean jackets. Did time for killing a rabid black dog, only he did the time on the left side of his brain! And he strayed, how he strayed. Became a team player. See the world sometimes when you're better off dead. *(Shakes head and body like a swimmer coming out of the water.)* Black Hole Buddy!

(Takes out harmonica. Plays two notes.) Now you know that I just wouldn't lie to you woman. Yeah, Baby—It's me. I'm Slide Blue Slim . . . *(Harmonica up. Cell phone out.)*

This baby stores something like 5,000 numbers in a chip the size of me when I got conceived. What's the chance of me finding one kind soul at the end of this line if I press a number—randomly? I say Slim . . . Slide Blue Slim . . . and so it goes. *(Pushes button on phone.)* Dial a pattern, intricate weaver. Ring—just a little bit. Ring, ring, ring . . .

JIMMY: *(Continued.)* Yeah? Who's this? . . . What? . . . Reichslin—Who? . . . Reichs, uh-man—I can't pronounce that! Who are you? . . . Tasarus—Huh? . . . Indonesian Restaurant in Amsterdam? . . . Amsterdam . . . Wait. Yeah—I know the place. Near Club 55.

(To self.) Why the hell would I keep this number?

(To phone.) What was that? . . . Who am I? *(Proudly.)* I'm Jimmy Shelter. Me and the band ate there a few times. We were on tour . . . The Ex-Laws, right! . . . Hey, what's wrong? . . .

(To self.) The guy's throwing a tantrum! Oh, shit! I remember. We trashed the joint our last night in town. Magnum threw up chunks of something in the fish tank and L.E. set fire to the bathroom . . .

(To phone.) Calm down, brother! What do you mean no one paid for the damages? . . . 13,000 Guilders? . . . How much is that? . . . 8,000 bucks? . . . What was the exchange rate then? . . . Take it easy. Of course I'm gonna pay. I'll send you a check, man. What's your address? . . . Hold on—The connection is slipping . . .

Hangs up laughing. LIMBO *sneaks into room. They know each other well.*

JIMMY: Slim, Slim . . . Slide Blue Slim. Of all the fucking numbers, I get that guy . . .

LIMBO: *(Menacing pose.)* Don't move.

JIMMY: *(Startled.)* Hey! *(Recognizes* LIMBO, *laughs.)* When did you get in?

LIMBO: It's "Check-Out Time."

JIMMY: Cool!

LIMBO: See it twice.

They shake hands.

JIMMY: Who you putting on, Man?

LIMBO: Replacement baseball player name a' Glen Scott Toby. The guys call me Costco 'cause I used to work there.

JIMMY: That's wild!

LIMBO: I'm a southpaw.

JIMMY: So what happens?

LIMBO: Well I'm a little guy living out his dreams, you know . . .

JIMMY: Yeah, Yeah—Poor little fuckers.

LIMBO: You got the picture.

JIMMY: Things don't work out.

Pause. JIMMY *takes out dropper bottle. Sniffs a few drops.*

JIMMY: Liquid methedrine and echinacea.

JIMMY *does a few more drops.*

JIMMY: What they got you on?

LIMBO *pulls out coke vial.*

LIMBO: Cocaine.

LIMBO *has a sniff.*

JIMMY: I hate that shit. Makes me too productive.

LIMBO: That can be a problem.

JIMMY: People start expecting . . . So?

LIMBO: When they settle the strike, I'm out of a job. Heard you had a new release.

JIMMY: Yep, Number 4 on the charts and climbing.

Pause.

JIMMY: When you start filming?

LIMBO: Mid-July. You do any more soundtracks?

JIMMY: Nah, SlaughterGate's the only one.

LIMBO *jumps up like he's holding a gun and throws his back to the wall.*

LIMBO: He's SlaughterGate! Come out, Ma—with your hands up!

JIMMY: I got the music!

LIMBO: Put it on.

JIMMY *puts on the instrumental soundtrack he did for the* GUY LIMBO *hit action movie, Slaughtergate.*

LIMBO: Alright, Ma—I'm coming in. Don't shoot! It's your son.

JIMMY: Your mom was crazy in that one!

LIMBO: Yeah . . . Like Ma Barker.

JIMMY: Right! *(Short pause.)* Who was Ma Barker?

LIMBO: She thought she was above the law. Shelley Winters played her in a Roger Corman film.

JIMMY: Who's Shelley Winters?

LIMBO: She died in *The Poseidon Adventure . . .*

Blackout.

Audio: Slaughtergate soundtrack continues.

Remove poster.

SCENE V:
Lily in a Chair

Slide appears with the word, "WEDNESDAY." Music and slide off. LILY *sits. Spotlight rises.*

LILY: Mother's stage name was Valencia. She sang with the USO. *(Sings.)* Kiss me once then kiss me twice . . . *(Drifts.)* I never knew my father . . . *(Pause.)*

Sweeny was an artist. He sold psychedelic posters. They met on the eve of the Summer of Love. Now, Gloria, you see—that's Sara's mom—ran off to California, to find herself . . . *(Pause.)*

I taught piano. Carl proposed to me after one of Sara's lessons. I mean, what else could the poor man do? There he was, all alone with a six-year-old daughter, and so I accepted. We were married in a chapel. I took care of Sara. Carl was so busy. He blew up in space on the Genesis II . . . *(Pause.)*

We didn't see Gloria until Carl's funeral. She brought her new husband, Sweeny along. They left a white dove on top of Carl's grave . . . *(Pause.)*

I grew up with Aunt Jean and my Uncle Joe. Mother travelled. She didn't know, either about my father, except he didn't like sailors and they met in a bar. That's all she remembered. That fellow, she told me, sure hated the sailors. Shipped out the next day to fight World War II . . . *(Pause.)*

You see, I married Sweeny, after Sara's mom died. She was killed at some concert. Oh, where? I've forgotten. Trampled to death. It was captured on film . . . *(Pause.)*

Once in a while, but not very often . . . I think I feel the need to belong where I've been. That's why I love to travel . . . *(Pause.)*

Gloria took Sara, soon after Carl died, so I followed them to San Francisco, minding Sara while the mother did her peace and love thing. And Sweeny, the husband? There we were, both widowed, so we brought up Sara. She was eight years old when Gloria died . . .

VOICEOVER DR. DEVILLE: Lily?

LILY: Yes, Doctor?

VOICEOVER DR. DEVILLE: Would you like another take?

Spotlight fades to black.

Audio: Sound of many clocks ticking; then ringing.

SCENE VI:
Sara's Room; Mid-Afternoon

During blackout, sound of clocks fades throughout voiceover.

VOICEOVER SARA: I don't want to hear about last week, Doctor.

VOICEOVER DR. DEVILLE: We got you that piece in *The Grapevine.*

VOICEOVER SARA: Whoop de do! Two measly columns on page 3 with no picture?

VOICEOVER DR. DEVILLE: What can I say? It's been a slow week. How does the cover of July's *GrooveSpin* grab you?

VOICEOVER SARA: Far out, Doctor! Now that's more like it.

VOICEOVER DR. DEVILLE: You want publicity, Sara? You get it. Come by my office and we'll schedule that interview. Hmm, that's funny— Your file's missing. Oh, I'll find it later. So, how are things going with you and Lily?

Pause. SARA *screams.*

Lights up.

Setting: SARA'S *room. Poster on wall reads: "Get High. Get Stupid. Get AIDS. Got Milk?"*

SARA *lies on bed munching out on a huge platter of candy. There's a bag of fan-mail in her room.*

SARA: *(Reading letter.)* Dear Ms. Kinetic, Love your show. Haven't missed one since my husband Bert died. Gratefully yours, Mrs. Evelyn Purdy . . . Idea for a pilot—Shades of Beckett. We see this woman watching TV. The music swells . . . "Waiting For Bert." *(Pause.)* Press agents are all bitches.

SARA: *(Talking to "press agent.")* What have you done for me lately?

SARA (AS AGENT):   You're in the TV Guide.

SARA: Oh, Goody! What page?

SARA (AS AGENT): 56. You're 31 down: talk show host "blank" Kinetic.

SARA: Crossword puzzles don't count, Creep! *(Pause.)* Hot Topic: Have you seen the punchbowl, Hon? Think about'em really—just lying around. Stored in some closet, used maybe once . . . Oh, Sara—You're being silly! Ta Ta, Ev! And the envelope please. *(Opens new letter.)* Sara Kinetic—You really excite me. I hope one day you'll visit my cell. *(Tosses letter.)* People who'd accomplish more in life behind bars . . .

Yah, Yah, Yah—Keep going, girl! Suicide Diet Doctors Guaranteed. Divorce Cases Involving Contract Killers. Supermodel Fashion Show's Crouton Cuisine. Tune in on Tomorrow—Today!

I made those punks at RVTV. Expanded the format. What about "Bar Search: The Weekly Battle of the Night Club Bands?" The new VJs suck. So what if they're young and their tits don't sag? Come on—Delilah Dooberry? Give me a break! She brought home a vibrator and chipped her teeth . . .

(Pause.)

Conversation with the Doctor—Part II, Part II: Look, DeVille—I want more copy. You got three weeks—or else! I'll open my own clinic and run you right out of the business! I'm Sara Kinetic—I call the shots!

LIMBO *sneaks in.*

LIMBO: Look Both Ways Before You Cross "The Deadline". . .

SARA: *(Unfazed.)* Hey, Blood and Guts—Shock treatment's down the hall.

LIMBO: I need something—an answer. It's falling apart.

SARA: Forgive me, but . . . *(Points.)* Stalk that way. And get out, mindfuck.

LIMBO: Are you really "THE" Ms. V.J. Sara One-and-Only Kinetic?

SARA: I know the racket, Bub. What's underneath?

LIMBO: *(Shuffles feet.)* Well, first of all, my name is Glen Scott Toby.

SARA: Jeepers by golly! Is this special, or what?

LIMBO: But the guys—well, see—They call me Costco.

SARA: Guys? What Guise?

LIMBO: I realized a dream playing big league ball.

SARA: And you really snapped a towel at another man's butt?

LIMBO: I traded my dreams for the system they built.

SARA: Good line, Roy. Okay I'm hooked. What? Spill.

LIMBO: Left-handed pitcher. Replacement baseball.

SARA: Pa could use some help, Son—down at the station.

LIMBO: The coaches were dealing, oh, drugs. You name it. Clean urine samples. I was under surveillance.

SARA: Test all kitchen magnets. Easiest place to plant a wire.

LIMBO: I'm running away from the pressure within.

SARA: And listen, Folks! Off the field he punches a clock!

LIMBO: Yeah—at Costco. I used to work at Costco.

SARA: The sight of you must've painted a smile on the face of every shopper.

LIMBO: This couple came in one time, and bought fifteen hampers. She looked like a role model, and the husband had to be about a foot and a half taller, with fifteen hampers!

SARA: Maybe they were transporting bootleg linen?

LIMBO: Never thought of that. Or White Slavers! Wicker baskets containing small, frightened children. That's cool!

SARA: Tell you what, Pal—I'll put you on the show. Wanna be the chair that nobody sits in?

LIMBO: I see—You're saying there's a chance to get it back.

SARA: It? What ? Dreams?

LIMBO: No. Reassurance. Immunity.

Pause.

SARA: So tell me. What? You like playing ball?

LIMBO: I like to be followed . . .

Blackout.

Audio: Loud applause begins.

Exit SARA *and* LIMBO.

Remove poster.

SCENE VII:
Activity Room; 3:30 p.m.

In blackout, LILY *sits on the couch watching back of TV. TV snow appears on screen facing audience.*

Audio: Applause fades.

TV VOICE 1: Kill the guy with the beedie.

TV VOICE 2: Why—That's manslaughter!

LILY: I don't understand.

Lights on.

JIMMY *enters looking fried.*

LILY: *(Pointing at TV.)* Look—

JIMMY: Hey—There's Lily. What's coming, Little Sister?

LILY: I think it's time for "Who Do You Love" or "CopWatch." I forget.

JIMMY: I wanna do a special with a buncha young bimbos. Call it "Neckfulla Hickies." Bring Pop Tarts . . .

LILY: I had a hickie once. My aunt didn't notice. The boy got lost— Like I wasn't there.

JIMMY: And all of them chewing gum.

LILY: I wouldn't let any of my students chew gum. I made them spit it out.

JIMMY: Yeah—we all got a lot to spit out.

Pause. JIMMY *pulls out harmonica.*

LILY: Do you like the rain?

JIMMY: Depends on the limo driver.

JIMMY *plays harmonica.*

JIMMY: *(Sings.)* What hotel in Kansas City? *(Stops.)* Do you sing?

LILY: Mother did. Look, Jimmy—Do you know this world?

JIMMY: Yes. And I sell what it does to my guts.

LILY: Then you see? That's best for you.

JIMMY: What's it like later?

LILY: I don't know. What was it before?

JIMMY: Freedom. Justice. And room to grow—

LILY: Marijuana?

JIMMY: No way, little sister!

LILY: I know. *(Laughs.)* I was making a joke.

JIMMY *looks at* LILY.

LILY: Didn't think the old lady had it in her, now did you?

JIMMY: I wrote a song you'd love called "Outer Body Neighbors." *(Stands. Sings.)* Walking the dog late at night in my dark . . . *(Pause.)* Why you here, Little Sister?

LILY: *(Points.)* I asked you first.

JIMMY: That's a good answer. Mind if I steal it? *(Whispers up at ceiling.)* You get that, Doc?

LILY: Sounds like you practice and preach.

JIMMY: We call that old preacher man Deacon Gestant—

LILY: See, I was right.

JIMMY: Wipe your nose.

LILY: It is "CopWatch."

JIMMY: *(Disenchanted.)* Ahh . . . They turn off the camera when someone gets shot.

Pause. Both watch the screen for a moment.

JIMMY: *(Points cellphone at* LILY *like a gun.)* Freeze, Little Sister! Say, I'm sliding. See me in your dreams.

JIMMY *exits.*

Audio: TV show "Copwatch."

TV ANNOUNCER: And now, tonight's letter to Copwatch.

TV LETTER WRITER (CONVICT): Dear Copwatch. I sure wanna thank ya'll for bustin' me live! You see, most cons lie about how they get caught. But ever since you showed me robbin' that fillin' station, I don't gotta. And the boys here treat me with respect. Signed, Ronald Lee Stone.

TV ANNOUNCER: Not actual voice.

During voiceover, LILY *sits back.* LIMBO *creeps into the room, testing the floor for landmines. He rolls over once and sits up with his legs out.*

LIMBO: Move quick. Walk tall. "Burn Proud."

LILY: You must represent the necessary evil!

LIMBO: Lady, you're right! That's been holding me back!

LILY: Plenty of time, but never to think.

LIMBO: *(Sits. Pause.)* What about residuals?

LILY: I don't have to worry.

LIMBO: Royalties?

LILY: Do you remember the Farrah Fawcett Major posters? My husband made them. Erik Estrada? I have no idea who these people were—but, still—I remember their names. *(Pause.)* You know, I've seen every one of your movies.

Blackout.

Audio: Drum solo begins.

Exit LIMBO *and* LILY.

SCENE VIII:
Jimmy's Room; Thursday, 1 p.m.

Audio: Drum solo continues.

Slide appears on USC *wall with the word "THURSDAY." After a moment, slide off.*

Enter JIMMY. *Set change to his room. Poster on wall reads "Helter Shelter."*

VOICEOVER DR. RATE: *(On intercom.)* Lily Gables-Sweeny, to Dr. Rate's office. Lily Gables-Sweeny—you're wanted, please.

Lights on.

JIMMY: *(On cellphone.)* What do you mean I don't love you anymore? Come on, Baby—I never loved you! No, I didn't love the Chinese girl either. *(Drums off.)* Nothing, just checking out drummers . . . No, there's nothing wrong with Magnum—Why? You fucking him, too? Great! I'm the only one . . . Okay, Paprika—Catch you later. *(Hangs up.)*

Girls, Girls, Girls! *(Pretends to seduce a young fan.)* Yeah, Baby—Let me show you. I'm you're daddy's worst nightmare . . . *(Sings.)* I'm you're daddy's worst nightmare!

SARA *knocks.*

JIMMY: Yeah?

SARA: What you doing?

JIMMY: Writing a song.

SARA: You're weird, Man.

JIMMY: Gotta keep my juices flowing.

SARA: I had this Bone Doctor on my show one time who said that women's bodies were colder than men's . . . *(Seductively.)* because of lower back extension. *(Pause.)* When are we going to get together, Jimmy?

JIMMY: I don't know.

SARA: Have you met this guy, Costco?

JIMMY: Who?

SARA: Costco—the baseball player?

JIMMY: Oh, him. He's my pal, Guy Limbo.

SARA: The movie star?

JIMMY: Comes here to get into his roles.

SARA: He doesn't look real.

JIMMY: The big screen distorts things.

SARA: What are you, some kind of prophet?

JIMMY: Yeah. *(Sings.)* Profito, the pirate, on a Spanish Galleon . . . waiting to ravage all the girls!

SARA: How do you remember all this stuff, if you don't write it down?

JIMMY: They record everything. That's why I come here. At the end of my stay I get everything packaged.

SARA: What's this? They're recording me right now?

JIMMY: I hope so! At least me. Well, that's what I'm paying them for. See, if I were out in the world I'd have to organize things all by myself. Find my own drugs. People always stop me on the street. So, like I said, they give me a package: Audio files. My words, my voice—liner notes, even. Then I just go home, press a button and listen. And that is how I write my songs.

SARA: I think I'll have a word with the good Doctor Rate. Who does that bitch think she is? Recording my voice without my permission. *(Turns to exit.)*

JIMMY: Hang loose, Kinetic. *(Grabs* SARA.*)* Hear my new tunes. *(Pulls her in closer.)* Who knows? Maybe you and I can still groove . . .

Blackout.

Audio: Echo-y part of "Whole Lotta Love" begins. Continue with rest of song.

Exit JIMMY *and* SARA.

Remove poster.

SCENE IX:
Dr. Rate's Office; Moments Later

Enter DR. RATE *and* LILY. RATE *stands.* LILY *sits* DS *from desk. Middle of "treatment."* LILY'S *purse is on the desk.* RATE *has a gun in the drawer.*

Audio fades. Lights up.

LILY: Are there any craft classes? You know, Doctor Rate—Some kind of diversion?

DR. RATE: Plenty to choose from. Take your pick. And, Lily—if you feel that none of them fulfill you, we'll start a new one to your specifications.

LILY: Why, that would be nice. Do we have a piano?

DR. RATE: A Baldwin baby grand.

LILY: Then I can play again?

DR. RATE: To your heart's content.

Pause. LILY *dreams.*

DR. RATE: Lily?

LILY: Hmm?

DR. RATE: I'd like to prescribe Thorate M.

LILY: Does that have Ginseng in it?

DR. RATE: It'll help you adapt.

LILY: I love the Orient. Fascinating people.

DR. RATE: Now—Lily, please. I'd like very much for you to stand in that corner.

LILY: Oh, Doctor, Have I been bad?

DR. RATE: Not at all. Just close your eyes. Make your mind a blank and I'll describe to you an image, then tell me the first word that comes to your mind.

LILY: *(Rises.)* Oh, dear me—A test!

DR. RATE: That's it. Now—there, please. Just relax. And make sure you close your eyes *(Puts the gun in* LILY's *purse.)* Okay, set. The image is: A square round of orange zero.

SARA *bursts into the office, still disheveled from her lovemaking session with* JIMMY.

SARA: I want to know what the hell's going on here, Doctor and I want to know—Now! Where's my file? I want to see my file! Something's going on and I intend to get to the bottom—or else! I'll have the crew from *Search and Seizure* here so fucking fast, it'll make your head spin!

DR. RATE: *(Removing folder.)* Well look, Sara, Why. Um. Here's your file!

LILY: *(Turns around.)* Honey, your bra's on backwards.

SARA: What's this I hear about you recording conversations?

LILY: They're putting me on Thorate M!

SARA: Hi, Lily.

LILY *waves.*

DR. RATE: Your imagination is getting the best of you, Sara. *(Pause.)* And now—Let's all hold hands and chant.

Blackout.

Audio: Chanting. Exit SARA, DR. RATE *and* LILY.

SCENE X:
Activity Room; Finale

Slide appears on USC *wall: "ONE WEEK LATER." After a moment, slide off.*

LIMBO *enters and lies on couch. TV snow appears.*

Audio: Chanting stops. TV baseball announcer begins. Lights rise on LIMBO.

TV ANNOUNCER: Bottom of the sixth . . . score tied at three . . . *(Continues for a while, then announcer morphs to* LIMBO'S *voice.)*

VOICEOVER LIMBO: Toby waits for the sign from Munson . . . Canseco at the plate . . . The moment you've all been waiting for, ladies and gentlemen . . . Glen Scott Toby . . . The guys call him Costco . . . What a story . . . The 1995 World Series . . . Game Seven . . . Top of the ninth . . . Toby picks up the rosin bag . . .

VOICEOVER DIRECTOR: Alright—cut! What the fuck happened, Limbo?

LIMBO: *(Live.)* What do you mean?

VOICEOVER DIRECTOR: I told you three times! Don't pick up the rosin bag until the batter steps up to the plate.

LIMBO: *(Live.)* But I thought—

VOICEOVER DIRECTOR: Don't! Just follow the script. We're over budget!

VOICEOVER LIMBO: *(Storming off set.)* Who's he think he is—pushing me around?

VOICEOVER BODYGUARD: What's wrong, Guy?

VOICEOVER DIRECTOR: I don't work like this, Limbo!

VOICEOVER LIMBO: Get that son of a bitch off my back, Charlie!

VOICEOVER BODYGUARD: Take it easy, Guy. Want me to turn on the radar gun?

Onstage, LIMBO *nods head at TV set.*

TV ANNOUNCER: And it's a base hit into left center field . . . Davis is rounding third . . . No, he holds up. Runners on first and third with nobody out . . .

LIMBO: *(Live.)* What would Costco do? Glen Scott Toby . . . Runners at the corners. The wind-up. The pitch—

TV ANNOUNCER: —And it's a home run! Ken Griffey, Jr. drives one deep into the bleachers.

LIMBO: *(Live)* Hey—in the script, I strike out the side!

VOICEOVER MOVIE CRITIC: And, now last and least, I give you the sleeper of the summer. I call this one a sleeper because that's what I was using my seat for as soon as this bomb starring Guy Limbo began. So, here's a clip from "Full Count"—Guy Limbo, in his first dramatic role. Should've stuck to shooting old ladies.

VOICEOVER *from "Full Count" script. Scene on the pitching mound.*

VOICEOVER ANDY: Throw him the curve, Costco! You can do it! Inside part of the plate!

VOICEOVER LIMBO: He's looking for the curve, Andy. Gimme something else!

VOICEOVER ANDY: Blow a fastball by him at the numbers!

VOICEOVER COSTCO AS ANNOUNCER: Munson settles in behind the plate. Canseco steps into the box. Toby picks up the rosin bag. The wind-up, and— *(Sound of huge explosion.)* It's a grenade! Toby threw a grenade! We'll see what the ump says when the smoke clears. Section 3 looks like a war zone! Wait—What's that? Out of the bullpen, looks like a motorcycle—with Rocket Launchers! Costco's in trouble! He's turning on the forcefield! And—Here Come The Helicopters . . .

VOICEOVER MOVIE CRITIC: Should've stuck to shooting old ladies.

LIMBO: *(Live.)* That's it! I can't do it! I won't do the film! I need Action! Danger! Bodybags . . .

Audio: Baseball announcer fades.

LIMBO: *(Holds "finger" gun.)* Okay, Row 8, Section 3. Call me a bum? Now say it with a gun to your head, Scumbag.

LIMBO *flips out shooting people in the stands.* JIMMY *enters dodging bullets.*

JIMMY: Chill out, Guy! Leave some kids to buy my albums.

LIMBO: I can't do it, man.

JIMMY: Do what?

LIMBO: The movie, "Full Count." Ain't my style. Director's a loser.

SARA *enters talking to* DR. DEVILLE.

DR. DEVILLE *carries a folder.*

Time for group therapy.

DR. DEVILLE: She's back next week. We'll straighten things out.

SARA: *(Walking past* LIMBO.*)* I know you! You're Guy Limbo! *(Sits. Takes up most of the couch.)* Where's Lily?

DR. DEVILLE: On the way. How you boys doing?

LIMBO: I'm not doing it, Doc. I'm not doing the picture.

DR. DEVILLE: Fine, fine . . . We must talk about that. Alright, everyone have a seat.

LILY *enters carrying a funny keychain with many attachments.*

Everyone speaks to her at once.

SARA: *(Whiny.)* Mom—
JIMMY: Little Sister—
LIMBO: Here's Lily—
DR. DEVILLE: Ah, There you are!

SARA: Where have you been?

LILY: Well, I'm taking a class. We make keychains, see? *(Holds out keychain.)* They gave me one. It's gold-plated. And this is a micro-metal detector . . .

JIMMY: *(Takes keychain.)* Far out!

LILY: We attach them.

JIMMY *hands keychain to* LIMBO.

LIMBO: Cool! Check the mail for bombs. *(Hands keychain back to* JIMMY.*)*

LILY: And, see—It has sun-screen, too!

JIMMY: Wow—the sunscreen—it's a dispenser! How much they want for this baby?

DR. DEVILLE: Okay, I'd like us now to focus on a new exercise.

SARA: It's exploitation of the masses.

LILY: And we answer the phone for this nice young man.

DR. DEVILLE: *(Sternly.)* And you run checks on the credit cards.

LILY: Oh, right, Doctor. We make sure the credit cards aren't stolen.

SARA: What time is it? My show's on!

LIMBO: *(To* JIMMY.*)* Let me see your phone.

JIMMY *hands his phone to limbo.* LIMBO *dials.*

LILY: Tomorrow, I think we're selling something for GreenPeace.

SARA: *(To* DR. DEVILLE.*)* Non-profit—no doubt.

DR. DEVILLE: *(Removing papers from folder.)* So why don't we all focus.

LIMBO: *(Frustrated.)* Line's busy. *(Keeps phone.)*

JIMMY: Maybe, I'll give Steeltoe a chance, if Magnum's out. He's the only one who remained true blue.

DR. DEVILLE: *(Hands out page to each.)* Here, now—Each of you take one. Lily, Sara. Jimmy. And Guy—one for you . . .

SARA: Today, Kinetic interviews Mighty Mouse. I talk to a cartoon, like Roger Rabbit.

DR. DEVILLE: Yes, I believe that would be most effective. You boys read, Part 1 aloud. Then, Lily and Sara? You read Part 2.

LILY: Is this like Row the Boat? Remember? In rounds?

JIMMY: Lily, you're a peach.

LIMBO: Doc, I forget—Is my part one or two?

DR. DEVILLE: I feel that this particular exercise exposes the absurdity of confrontation. Okay, Part 1—

JIMMY *reads;* LIMBO *chimes in.*

JIMMY AND LIMBO: My daddy was killed in Haiti! I'll kick your ass!

DR. DEVILLE: Now, Number 2.

SARA AND LILY: I was in the big one—Granada! We used three cans of K-rations!

DR. DEVILLE: Again! Guy . . . Jimmy!

JIMMY AND LIMBO: My daddy was killed in Haiti! I'll kick your ass!

DR. DEVILLE: Girls . . .

LILY: I was in the big one—

SARA: Wait! *(Grabs remote.)* Time for my show!

Audio: Begin commercial.

TV ANNOUNCER: If you use Clorazine breath spray . . .

LILY: That's my brand!

LILY *reaches into her purse for breath spray and finds gun. She holds the gun with her pinkie out.*

TV ANNOUNCER: You'll need Voice Mail with Call Waiting . . .

DR. DEVILLE: I believe we can take a little break.

LIMBO *dials phone.*

TV ANNOUNCER: The regularly scheduled program will not be seen, so we may bring you the following special.

SARA: What's going on?

LIMBO: Still busy.

JIMMY: Maybe someone got shot.

SARA: Where's my show?

DR. DEVILLE: *(Along with TV.)* As I said, the point of this exercise is to unhinge our free will from the stereotypical responses which we're bombarded with each and every day by the media, by our friends and neighbors, by parents, co-workers . . . *(Sees DR. RATE on the TV.)*

TV ANNOUNCER: Good Afternoon, and welcome once again to "Get A Grip—Results from the Power of Choice." With your host, The Advice Broker—

LILY: *(Points gun at TV.)* Look!

TV ANNOUNCER: Doctor Amelia Rate.

DR. DEVILLE: Amelia?

SARA: Rate?

JIMMY: Amelia? Wow! Her name's Amelia! *(Takes out harmonica.)*

SARA: I knew the sneaky bitch had something up her sleeve.

LIMBO: *(On phone.)* Look, Weinberg. I'm not doing the picture . . . Break the contract . . . Okay, then I'm calling Maxwell direct. *(Hangs up. Dials.)*

JIMMY: *(Plays harmonica.)* Making love in the afternoon, with Amelia up in my bedroom . . .

TV DR. RATE: Thank you for joining us here in the studio. Our Get A Grip Touchstone Topic today—Women who never once had their period . . .

SARA: *(Throws a fit.)* Why the cunt even stole my idea!

JIMMY: I got up to wash my face, when I come back again—Oh, she's taking my place.

DR. DEVILLE: Hmmm . . . She'll be hard to replace. *(Caresses plant.)* How's my little baby?

LIMBO: *(On phone.)* Sorry, Maxwell . . . I can't do the picture.

SARA *continues tantrum.* LILY *(divided) points gun between TV and* SARA.

TV DR. RATE: Also, today—Ms. Mag Delain, whose throat bleeds three days a month . . .

SARA: They take you . . . All skin and bones . . . And wrap you in a neat little package. Some daddy girl, mom apple eye. No choice built-in but to be loved. And to what world would her dream go? With choice and will, she could be loved . . . *(Pause.)*

I was born picked clean, and I can't get back. So I ain't coming out . . . *(Places pillow over head.)* Ever.

LILY *crosses and holds the gun to* SARA'S *pillow, and fires. Then she crosses back and looks at the television.*

LIMBO *stares in shock, then returns to phonecall.* JIMMY *stops singing, looks, and sits at the end of couch.* DEVILLE *turns from plant and stares at* LILY.

LIMBO: *(On phone.)* Hey, Prado—Look—They want to see action. Bullet holes. We got —what?—40, 50 thousand people sitting in the stands? Gimme an Uzi. Let me kill some of them. Just ten— maybe 12 . . . I'll save the rest. Get back to me. *(Hangs up.)*

DR. DEVILLE: *(Crosses to* LILY.*)* Lily, Lily . . . Can you fathom the enormous step you've just taken in your life? You were able to feel something deep down inside and act decisively upon that feeling. *(Leads* LILY *offstage.)* How does it feel?

LILY: Everything should always be perfect . . .

DR. DEVILLE: Fine, fine . . . Let's go to my office and call an attorney. I know a few—but they'll cost.

LILY: Money's no object.

DR. DEVILLE: Fine, fine . . . Money's no object.

LIMBO: *(Hands* JIMMY *phone.)* I broke off the deal, man. Costco's done. *(Takes out cocaine.)*

JIMMY: *(Sings.)* Mother Mary Drove the Nails into Little Baby Jesus.

LIMBO: *(Holds out vial.)* Guess I won't be needing this.

JIMMY: Hey, now. *(Takes vial.)* What the fuck, Guy. You see? *(Unscrews cap.)* I think it's time for a change.

JIMMY *wanders off the stage snorting cocaine.* LIMBO *follows, stops at the door and puts his back to the wall.*

LIMBO: *(Holds out hand like gun; checks room.)* The Fruit of All Evil . . . Utopia . . . Coming soon to a theater near you . . .

Blackout.

Exit LIMBO.

SARA *removes pillow, then sits up and rubs blood on her face.*

EPILOGUE:
The Play's the Thing

Video of the cast (excluding SARA*), as if they were talking live in the dressing room after a performance. This time, the video is actually shown to the audience. During video, blue light rises on* SARA*, still on couch, watching the TV with blood on her face: cackling, laughing, carrying on.*

DR. DEVILLE: We're going to do the infomercial now!

DR. RATE: We are not doing the infomercial!

JIMMY: Jimmy Shelter has left the building!

DR. DEVILLE: Who needs a cure for life?

JIMMY: You see that guy in the front row jump when you shot the gun?

LILY: Hey! I jumped when I shot the gun!

JIMMY: They loved it!

LILY: It was a beautiful thing.

DIRECTOR: *(Rushing into dressing room.)* Shhh! Be quiet! The audience can hear you!

LILY: God willing . . .

LIMBO: *(Holding vial up to camera.)* Dude—I used real coke.

Video ends. Onstage lights fade to black.

Audio: Rolling Stones' "Star Star."

Curtain call: Cast on stage—Bows, then turns to hidden onstage camera and waves, which shows up on the TV. Exit cast.

Lights on audience. TV shows the AUDIENCE*, shot from hidden camera on stage.*

THE END

HUNGER

A Play Inspired by the Knut Hamsun Novel

The Fantasy Consumes Itself

PRODUCTION NOTES:

The main character of Knut Hamsun's novel, *Hunger*, is a starving young writer. Having read the book many times in my teens, I was compelled to be as unpragmatic as Hamsun's protagonist when it was my turn. Thus—this semi-auto-bio-cum-homage to the novel.

When faced with staging *Hunger*, one directive came to light: The play must be performed by an all-female cast. The reason for this is twofold:

1. This relieves an audience of the need to judge it in any way sexist; and

2. It was time to give the ghosts of theater past (casting only men for centuries) a taste of their own medicine—Sexist Bastards!

(See what I mean.)

—*P.C.*

HUNGER

SETTING:

BILLIE *the writer's cheap furnished room.* SR: *An unmade bed, a desk and chair.* USC: *A small dresser, below a curtained window.* SL: *A door with a peephole, and a closet in the upstage corner.*

BILLIE'S *image stares out from a mirror hung above the desk with a typewriter. An old radio on the headboard plays jazz. Books and papers are strewn about. Onstage lights up low before play begins.*

CHARACTERS:

BILLIE: *30-year-old starving writer.*
Also: LATIMER: *Convict. Killed his mom.*
             HARRY: *A hesitant John.*

SAMANTHA: BILLY'S *girl.*
Also: BLANCHE: *Transvestite from the street.*
             ONE & TRES: *1st part and 3rd piece.*

INDIGO: LATIMER'S *fantasy girl/guy.*
Also: SUZY: *Rocker girl.*
             TWO & DOS: *2nd part and 2nd piece.*

HONEYSUCKLE: *Underground Atlantis hooker.*
Also: CHERYL: *Rocker girl.*
             THREE & UNO: *3rd part and 1st piece.*

SCENE I

Onstage lights fade to black. BILLIE *enters and lays spreading supine on bed. Music fades as blue bed light rises—low.*

BILLIE *is lying at 12 o'clock position on bed.*

BILLIE: Let's see . . . Things I gotta do today . . .

Pause. Mirror light rises.

Inspire myself . . .

Turns head SR—*looks at mirror. Mirror light off sharp.* BILLIE *laughs, Turns head back.*

That's a good one . . .

Looks SL *at door; turns head back. Puts hands behind head.*

What else I gotta do today?

Music rises slowly as blue bed light fades.

SCENE II

BILLIE *crouches, typing, trying to create. Leans in—stares at title. Music continues. Room lights up sharp.*

BILLIE: Fire in the Bookstore . . . *(Pause.)* Too fucking lame . . . Too fucking Nazi . . . Had to be more—than two fucking Nazis . . . Make a note. Find out—exactly—how many fucking Nazis there were . . . *(Looks at door—shows concern. Leans in—stares at title.)* Fire—Forget it! *(Yanks out piece of paper.)* I can do better . . . *(Balls up paper —stands.)*

How 'bout a nickname—Like . . . something . . . Like something . . . *(Turns off radio—music off.)* What? Saint . . . *(Smiles.)* Saint-Saint-Saint, Impulse? *(Pause.)* I like it . . . *(Sits at desk; inserts new page—types.)*

Saint Impulse . . .

Wait! Who was that guy? *(Picks up book.)* Killed his mother for insurance—uhm . . . Latimer. Here we go . . . Strangled his ma. *(Pause.)*

So what makes Latimer Saint Impulse? He's a prisoner—aren't we all? Nah . . . Let's see. Sentenced to life in 1886 . . . Learned to cook—then, as a joke . . . poisoned two guards. One died, but— what the hay? That rascal was forgiven. Seems Latimer—Saint Impulse—was voted most popular con. And . . .

Right—This is it! In 1926, They . . . built a better prison, but Latimer was unprepared to leave his happy home. So, he begged them to stay, and somehow his wish was granted. Wow. *(Closes book; stands—crossing to foot of bed.)* Somebody in the penal system left him there—alone—as the caretaker . . . *(Turns to desk.)* Kept his old cell and everything . . .

Room lights fade.

BILLIE *changes into* LATIMER.

SCENE III

Scene change: Room to cell. USC *curtain opens revealing barred window. Small dresser becomes bunk.*

Audio: Music fades.

LATIMER: Ladies and gentlemen . . .

Cell light up sharp.

LATIMER: Kids! Welcome to Tartarus State Prison, which once housed . . . Housed? I don't like it. Held, Yeah—Held. Which once held over 500 desperate men. This is D block and the cell right here has been my home going on 41 years. Latimer here, Saint Impulse. I'm the caretaker, and today I'll be your guide— Follow me . . . *(Pause.)*

Please, God, Let me stay! Please, Mr. Warden! I'll make you proud . . . I know they'll let me stay— Wait! Who's gonna cook my meals? Good question. Make a note. How do I eat? No problem—I'm not such a bad cook . . . if I may be bold enough to say. And believe me, I'm bold enough. Been around killers and thieves most a my life and look at me now . . . *(Pause.)*

Okay . . . I killed ma . . . needed the money—Wait! Where's the food gonna come from? Make a note. Ask about food. And cleaning supplies . . . *(Pause.)*

One day, I'll get out, and find the place where I buried the cats and dogs. 100 dollar bills and fifties folded neatly. Sewed 'em up inside 'em myself. Rover, Queenie . . . Mom's little black poodle, Jo-Jo—yap-yap . . . God, I hated that fucking animal . . . Bit me on the forehead once . . . got 300 bucks stashed inside the little fucker . . . *(Looking up—pleads desperately.)* Oh—Please let me stay! *(Quickly recomposes.)* And the cats . . . *(Pause—peers out cell window.)* I'll find them when I'm free . . . Free . . . Ahhh . . . All of us are prisoners, inside or out. Money . . . Money . . . Rover, Queenie. Hey, Ma! Can you hear me? I killed you Ma—and for that I'm sorry . . . *(Pause.)*

LATIMER: *(Continued.)* And the guard. Gave him too much poison. Now, people—I'm real sorry about the guard. I didn't mean to kill him. It was just a joke. The other one only got sick—Wait! What if I'm the one who gets sick?

LATIMER *closes eyes—manifesting* INDIGO, *his fantasy girl—who enters behind him like magic.*

INDIGO: I'll take care of you. I'll do everything.

LATIMER: *(Opens eyes. Turns to* INDIGO.*)* You're late.

INDIGO: I wore the nice blue thing you like.

LATIMER: Look, Indigo—Once I'm caretaker here, I won't have time for your bullshit.

INDIGO: Okay, you old grump. What do you want me to do?

LATIMER: *(Points at bench.)* Sit down. I want you to take some dictation.

INDIGO *sits with pencil and paper in hand.*

LATIMER: No—Stand up. I want to hear you read my speech out loud.

INDIGO *stands and poses sexy.*

LATIMER: Pick up the fucking papers!

INDIGO *picks up the papers.*

LATIMER: *(Sits.)* Start on page two—second paragraph.

INDIGO: *(Reads.)* It was only a joke. I didn't mean to kill the guard— *(Fawning.)* Did you really kill a guard?

LATIMER: Can the wisecracks and read.

INDIGO: *(Sits.)* Latimer . . . Saint Impulse—Let's have a baby.

LATIMER: *(Groans.)* Again with this crap . . . What did I tell you?

INDIGO: Well, one night—remember?—you whispered in my ear, Indigo, I want a baby.

LATIMER: Yeah Yeah Yeah. Thanks, but no thanks. *(Stands.* INDIGO *rises behind him.)* Hey, Ma! You listening? Gave me life and got strangled in the process. Why inflict more torture? *(Slaps* INDIGO.*)*

Pause.

INDIGO: *(Unfazed.)* Want me to read?

LATIMER: When we get out you can help me find the pets.

INDIGO: What pets?

LATIMER: Kittycats. And the dogs. I never told you about my dogs—Rover and Queenie . . . *(They sit.)* Sewed a bunch of money under their skin. Mom's poodle Jo-Jo—

INDIGO: The one that bit you on the forehead?

LATIMER: Kicked it clear across the room. Now shut up and read. Top of page 3. I need some time to think things out.

INDIGO *stands shuffling papers.*

INDIGO: Here we are, folks—The electric chair. And death row is to your right . . .

LATIMER: You see, I figure—the first thing we do is show 'em the chair. Then the crowd's happy. They tell all their friends. Okay—Keep going . . .

INDIGO: Uh-oh!

LATIMER: What—Lose your place?

INDIGO: Uh-huh. I lost it—listening to you.

Pause.

INDIGO: *(Sits.)* Sorry.

LATIMER: *(Smiles.)* One for Mom.

INDIGO: Sorry, Mom.

LATIMER: Sorry, Ma.

INDIGO: Tell me about the dogs again and what we're gonna do when we get out. I just love the sound of your voice.

LATIMER: Okay, look—First we find the place where the dogs're buried, then we dig 'em all up and get the dough,

INDIGO: What about the cats?

LATIMER: Don't get cute!

INDIGO: Out there, we'd face only disappointment.

LATIMER: *(Rises.)* I'll find them.

INDIGO: *(Kneels.)* Take me with you.

LATIMER: I'll think about it.

INDIGO: *(Pleading.)* But!

LATIMER: Now read! Top of page 4—and speak up! You never enunciate your words properly.

INDIGO: *(Proudly front and center, page in hand.)* The new breed of badmen, nowadays, folks—well—they ain't got the class of the old time criminal. *(Pause.)* Listen . . .

Cell light out sharp. Jazz music rises.

Exit INDIGO. LATIMER *changes back to* BILLIE.

SCENE IV

Scene change: Cell to room. BILLIE *has been telling the story of* LATIMER *to* SAMANTHA. *She lies in bed half-dressed.* BILLIE *sits by the typewriter.*

BILLIE: *(Eagerly awaiting* SAMANTHA'S *opinion.)* So?

Room lights up sharp.

SAMANTHA: *(Turns off radio.)* I don't see why he has to abuse her.

BILLIE: Baby . . . It's all in his mind.

SAMANTHA: I'm worried about you. When's the last time you ate?

BILLIE *throws* SAMANTHA *a sly look.*

SAMANTHA: You're avoiding the question.

BILLIE: An impulse "evolves" from the hunger within.

SAMANTHA: Meaning?

BILLIE: All of it, Samantha—Everything. Meaning why you're in this room with me.

SAMANTHA: And with this, you promote violence against women?

BILLIE: I'm not promoting anything. Would you like my story better if the lady goes outside and plants her bulbs before spring?

SAMANTHA: Okay, Billie. Some parts were funny. Where'd you get the idea for the dogs and cats?

BILLIE: Dead bodies are the only tangible vestige to his past.

SAMANTHA: Smooth that out for me, please.

BILLIE: The guy was lonesome . . . So I gave him a fantasy girl.

SAMANTHA: This room is too dark . . . and it smells like cigarettes.

BILLIE: So the mystique of the starving artist is a hoax is it?

SAMANTHA: I just think you'd be more productive if you had a better place.

BILLIE: *(Climbs into bed.)* Okay. I'll move in with you.

SAMANTHA: What about Kevin?

BILLIE: I thought it was over.

Pause.

SAMANTHA: What am I going to do with you?

BILLIE: Rhetorically speaking?

SAMANTHA: Seems to me—

There's a knock on the door.

SAMANTHA: Expecting someone?

BILLIE: *(Rises.)* Maybe it's the old man.

SAMANTHA: What old man?

BILLIE: *(Moving to the door.)* The one always sitting in the lobby.

SAMANTHA: You owe him money?

BILLIE: Nah. *(Looks through peephole.)* Uh-oh . . . *(Backs off.)* Look— It's Elaine.

SAMANTHA: Really.

BILLIE: *(Sits.)* Shit. I can't let her in.

SAMANTHA: What am I doing here?

There's a second knock. They sit in silence, then BILLIE *crosses to the door.*

BILLIE: *(Staring through peephole.)* She's gone . . .

SAMANTHA: Why don't you run after her?

BILLIE: What?

SAMANTHA: Run after her. Bring her back.

BILLIE: What about you?

SAMANTHA: Well? What about me?

BILLIE: I don't know—you tell me . . . *(Sings.)* You gotta . . . Tell me you're coming . . . back to me . . . You gotta . . .

SAMANTHA: Kevin plays that on the guitar.

BILLIE: Maybe he'll show up next.

SAMANTHA: I don't think so.

BILLIE: I don't think so . . .

Pause. BILLIE *sits on the floor* DSR.

SAMANTHA *takes her shirt off the back of the chair, starts to get dressed.*

BILLIE: Where do you think you're going?

SAMANTHA: She might come back, Billie.

BILLIE: Come on . . . Stick around . . . To the victor goes the spoils.

SAMANTHA: *(Corrects* BILLIE.*)* Go.

BILLIE: What?

SAMANTHA: Go. To the victor "go" the spoils.

BILLIE: Oh . . .

Pause.

SAMANTHA: I think you're the one that needs the fantasy girl.

BILLIE: *(Climbs into bed.)* You're my fantasy girl.

SAMANTHA: Saint Bullshit.

BILLIE: Hey, Samantha—If you leave, you won't have me to kick around anymore. Then you'll have to criticize yourself . . .

SAMANTHA: Go back to your story.

BILLIE: I've got a new one. Underground Atlantis. See—They find the lost city of Atlantis off the coast of San Diego, and —

SAMANTHA: *(Points to story in the typewriter.)* Saint Impulse?

BILLIE: —turn it into a vice-ridden den. *(Pause. Leans back on bed.)*

SAMANTHA: *(Leaning back on bed—turns radio on.)* You know, you'd be better off if you had a computer . . .

Room lights fade. Music rises. Exit SAMANTHA.

BILLIE *changes into* HARRY.

SCENE V

Scene change: Room becomes Underground Atlantis. SL *corner closet folds open to expose a small room with aquarium motif, and a giant TV monitor, with a chair on each side of monitor.* HONEYSUCKLE *sits in* SL *chair. An empty chair awaits* HARRY, *who stands a few steps away from it.*

Audio: Music fades.

HONEYSUCKLE: Come on . . . Sit down. Don't be shy . . .

Underground Atlantis lights up sharp.

HARRY: I've never done anything like this before.

HONEYSUCKLE: What's your name?

HARRY: Harry.

HONEYSUCKLE: Don't worry, Harry—I will bite. Welcome to Underground Atlantis. My name's Honeysuckle, and I want you bad—

HARRY: *(Corrects her.)* —"ly" . . .

HONEYSUCKLE: What?

HARRY: I want you "bad-ly."

HONEYSUCKLE: Oh. Are you a writer?

HARRY: Uh—I don't have to be a writer, well . . . Yeah—I'm a writer.

HONEYSUCKLE: I knew it.

HARRY: *(Sits.)* Can I ask you a question?

HONEYSUCKLE: Shoot.

HARRY: Where's the bed?

HONEYSUCKLE: Want some hot talk, Harry? Huh? What do you want?

HARRY: I don't know yet. I'm trying to feel this thing out.

HONEYSUCKLE: *(Spreads legs.)* Why don't you feel this thing out . . .

HARRY: Why are you doing this? You're so beautiful . . .

HONEYSUCKLE: Harry, baby—That's why I'm doing it. I'm gonna make you happy.

HARRY: Is that love?

HONEYSUCKLE: What?

HARRY: This.

Pause.

HONEYSUCKLE: Do you write about sad things, Harry?

HARRY: I guess so . . .

HONEYSUCKLE: I get all sad—you know, when I see animals locked up in a zoo.

Pause.

HONEYSUCKLE: You gonna write about me, Harry?

HARRY: Probably . . .

HONEYSUCKLE: Will it be sad?

HARRY: No, Honeysuckle . . . It won't be sad.

Pause.

HONEYSUCKLE: I like those nature shows on TV—you know—the ones where you get to see animals lying around, licking their claws with their eyes half-closed. *(Pause.)* I'd hate to be locked up.

HARRY: So you like your work?

HONEYSUCKLE: The food's good. I can eat steak every night!

HARRY: What about lobster?

HONEYSUCKLE: I hate seafood!

HARRY: *(Laughs.)* I was married to a woman who hated seafood.

HONEYSUCKLE: You were married?

HARRY: *(Nods.)* The therapist told her that hating seafood was self-deprecating . . . So, how do we go about this thing?

HONEYSUCKLE *embraces the large monitor.*

HONEYSUCKLE: Harry? Do you have a major credit card?

Underground Atlantis lights off sharp. Jazz music rises. Exit HONEYSUCKLE.

HARRY *changes back to* BILLIE.

SCENE VI

Scene change: Underground Atlantis to BILLIE'S *room; corner closet folds back. Mirror light rises.*

BILLIE *is lying at 9 o'clock position on bed.*

BILLIE: To arouse a desire to create is difficult . . .

Pause.

To kill that desire . . . is easy.

Mirror light fades.

Audio: Sound of door closing. Jazz music continues.

SCENE VII

SUZY *and* CHERYL *are in* BILLIE*'s room.* BILLIE *met them at the bar.*

CHERYL: Is this where bums live?

Room lights up sharp.

BILLIE: *(Drunk—staring through peephole; backs off.)* He wasn't there.

SUZY: I think one of the addicts lives upstairs.

CHERYL: She works in a methadone clinic.

BILLIE: *(To* CHERYL.*)* What do you do?

CHERYL: I — . . . *(Hiccups.)*

BILLIE: *(Laughing.)* What?

CHERYL: I — . . . *(Hiccups.)*

SUZY: She works for AT&T.

CHERYL: *(Recovering.)* Accounts receivable.

BILLIE: Haven't seen you gals around the bar before.

CHERYL: We're staying at her sister's.

SUZY: She's a stewardess.

BILLIE: *(To* CHERYL.*)* You got any sisters, Suzy?

CHERYL: I'm Cheryl! *(Pointing.)* That's Suzy.

SUZY: *(Offended.)* I'm Suzy.

BILLIE: Right, Right . . . Suzy—Cheryl, Suzy—Cheryl. Sorry.

CHERYL: I've got 2 sisters.

SUZY: I smoked 3 cigarettes tonight.

CHERYL: And you had a shot of tequila. I can't drink tequila. I get the hiccups.

SUZY: What's this music?

BILLIE: Jazz. I like it . . .

CHERYL: Can we change it?

SUZY *spins the radio dial.*

BILLIE: Be my guest.

Nirvana's "Smells Like Teen Spirit" comes on.

CHERYL: *(Dancing.)* Who's this?

BILLIE: I wouldn't know.

SUZY: Nirvana.

CHERYL: Me and Suzy went to our first concert together.

BILLIE: So you two went to the same school and all?

SUZY: *(Starts dancing.)* Yeah . . .

CHERYL: It was sold out.

SUZY: *(To BILLIE.)* Did you ever see The Beatles?

BILLIE: Nah . . . I was too young to see The Beatles.

CHERYL: I met a guy once who saw The Beatles. He was getting ready to produce their reunion album when John Lennon got killed. I went home with him, but his hot tub was broken.

BILLIE *laughs and grabs notebook to write* CHERYL's *line down. New rock and roll song begins.*

CHERYL: Hey! This is our favorite!

SUZY: What do you write about?

BILLIE: Oh . . . I've got this one story about a prisoner who abuses his fantasy girl.

SUZY: My sister married a guy that beat her up. They went to therapy and he stopped. Then she left him.

BILLIE: You think that's because he stopped hitting her?

SUZY: *(Crossing to* CHERYL.*)* She's in Montreal.

SUZY *whispers to* CHERYL

CHERYL: Suzy said something that you might have some drugs?

BILLIE: Well . . . There's a pint of vodka here, somewhere. *(Finds bottle.)* Want some?

CHERYL: Yeah . . . *(Takes a sip.)*

BILLIE: Suzy?

SUZY: I don't drink hard liquor.

CHERYL: Do you mind if we jump on the bed?

SUZY: *(Leaping onto bed first.)* Come on Cheryl!

CHERYL *hiccups, jumps on bed and dances with* SUZY.

BILLIE: *(Walking around bed.)* Their journey evidently has no end . . . *(Pause.)* They look like humping insects . . . determined to make a place for themselves in the world . . .

Room lights off sharp. BILLIE *sits and types.*

Exit SUZY *and* CHERYL.

SCENE VIII

BILLIE'S *room an hour later. Rock music stops abruptly.* BILLIE *sits at desk.*

BILLIE: Reality contaminates . . . the substance which "inspires" . . .

Room lights up sharp.

BILLIE: *(Creating.)* Another dry-shit clown mask pasted on a brand new Chrysler . . . *(Pause.)* Bought over the counter at your local discussion.

Center lights rise. ONE, TWO *and* THREE *enter carrying their respective body mask casts, which they set down facing audience.*

TWO: Number Three was late again.

ONE: Number Three?

THREE: My car was sick—I mean I was sick. Number Two was blocking my way.

ONE: Number Two?

TWO: Number Three was late again.

ONE: Number Three? The charge is loitering.

THREE: Inspiration has its own time.

TWO: A blank lie.

THREE: For what gain?

ONE: Get to the point.

BILLIE: *(Types.)* Get to the point . . .

ONE, TWO & THREE: *(All.)* The world's screwed up.

BILLIE: And each soul must manipulate . . . in order to survive.

ONE: Number Two?

TWO *rises to attention.*

ONE: On your report next to Disciplinary Action Needed, you wrote Number Two.

TWO: I'm sorry Number One. I meant Number Three.

ONE: Other companies have toppled from smaller mistakes. Pay attention. *(Pause.)* Number Three?

THREE *rises to attention.*

ONE: Where's your report?

THREE: I don't have one.

ONE: Why not?

THREE: Because if I had my report, nothing would be wrong . . . and then you'd have to criticize yourself.

BILLIE *rips paper from typewriter.*

BILLIE: Not bad. What next? Uhhhh—

ONE, TWO & THREE: *(Together.)* Fire in the bookstore?

BILLIE: Nah—I can do better.

ONE: Meeting adjourned.

Center lights fade. ONE, TWO & THREE *exit offstage. Body casts remain.*

BILLIE: So, I got one sick side of the dark venal world. Now—Ram it in and break it off. Switch One and Three and bring in the clean up crew.

UNO, DOS *and* TRES *enter.* ONE *is* TRES; THREE *is* UNO *and* TWO *is* DOS.

DOS: *(Whispering to* UNO.*)* Tres is getting evicted.

TRES: Hey, Uno—I need some time off next week. My family's getting evicted.

UNO: No can do, Tres. We're too busy. Move your family at night.

DOS: *(Whispering to* TRES.*)* That Uno is a tough son of a bitch.

UNO: What did you say, Dos?

DOS: Uh—Nothing, Boss. Just cleaning Number Two.

UNO: Yeah? Well keep on cleaning Number Two. I've been getting unsatisfactory reports about this office as of late.

TRES: *(Cleaning cast of* ONE.*)* You know, I kinda look like Number One.

UNO: Well Number One ain't the one whose getting evicted, Tres!

DOS: Uno looks like Number Three.

DOS *and* TRES *snicker.*

UNO: Dos! Don't press your luck. Hmmm . . . I wonder what it's like to be the one on top . . . *(Pause.)* Dos?

DOS *and* TRES *rise to attention.*

DOS: Tres was late again.

UNO: Tres?

TRES: My car was sick—I mean I was sick. Dos was blocking my way.

UNO: Yep . . . That's just about how I thought it would be . . . *(Takes* THREE's *cast.)* Okay, you two—Let's clean his room. *(Dances off.)*

DOS: *(Takes* TWO's *cast.)* Pick up those fucking papers—Dos! *(Dances off.)*

TRES: *(Takes* ONE's *cast.)* And Tres—You make the bed! *(Dances off.)*

BILLIE: I sit here prey to the weirdest fantasies . . .

Music rises. BILLIE *climbs into bed. Lights fade to black.*

SCENE X

Mirror light rises.

Audio: "Flamenco Sketches" by Joe Henderson.

BILLIE *is lying at 6 o'clock position on bed.*

BILLIE: Sometimes your eyes shine . . .

Ever so like flowers . . .

I'm head over heels in love with you . . .

What is your name?

Mirror light fades.

SCENE XI

Music continues. Sound of door closing. BLANCHE *is with* BILLIE. *They met on the street.*

BILLIE: I don't believe it! I go out to get the paper at this ungodly hour and find you on the corner instead . . .

Room lights up sharp.

BLANCHE: This room is bigger than mine.

BILLIE: *(Taking off his coat.)* And you really live in this building?

BLANCHE: Third floor.

BILLIE: I don't believe it! And your name is Blanche?

BLANCHE: With a "b" as in "boy."

BILLIE: I'm a saint, Blanche—I'm a saint . . . *(Pause.)* What are you doing on the street? You're so beautiful . . .

BLANCHE: That's what I'm doing on the street, Saint.

BILLIE: *(Hanging his coat on the back of the chair.)* Sunday morning? It's dead out there. Want some vodka? *(Finds the bottle empty.)* Aww . . . Sit down . . . *(Pause.)* I'm glad you came back with me . . .

BLANCHE *sits on the edge of the bed.*

BILLIE *sits on the floor next to* BLANCHE.

BILLIE: *(To himself).* Can't find nothing til 5 in the morning . . . Hey, Blanche? Do you—always—rely on the kindness of strangers?

BLANCHE: When I enter certain places, I can sense things.

BILLIE: Oh yeah?

BLANCHE: I'm sort of psychic.

BILLIE: Well, I'm a saint. Think we got a chance?

BLANCHE: Other times I'm a bandleader.

Pause.

BILLIE: Hey! He wasn't out there . . .

BLANCHE: Who?

BILLIE: The old man that sits in the lobby . . . He wasn't there . . . Maybe he died in his sleep . . . .

Pause.

BILLIE: *(Stands.)* So . . . Is this all you know?

BLANCHE: What? Selling my body?

BILLIE: I mean, well—You shouldn't . . .

Pause.

BLANCHE: So what do you do?

BILLIE: I'm a writer.

BLANCHE: How do you live?

BILLIE: Uh—collect unemployment.

BLANCHE: What'd you do before?

BILLIE: Show up late for some shit job . . . *(Pause.)* Look, Blanche, I got about six or seven bucks—Here. You take it. Just stay off the street . . . You're too good for that . . .

Pause.

BLANCHE: *(Crosses to desk and sits in chair.)* So you just write down whatever comes into your head?

BILLIE: *(Laughs to himself.)* Yeah, always something rolling around up there . . .

BLANCHE: You gonna write about me?

BILLIE: Yeah, Honeysuckle.

BLANCHE: What did you call me?

BILLIE: Oh, nothing . . .

BLANCHE: Saint?

BILLIE: Blanche . . .

BLANCHE: Do you know what am I?

BILLIE: Sure . . .

BLANCHE: I'm a man.

BILLIE: You're a wonderful person . . .

BLANCHE: Hey—Saint . . .

BILLIE: You're beautiful . . .

BLANCHE *kneels before* BILLIE *at the foot of the bed.*

BLANCHE: Tell me what you want.

Room light fades. BLANCHE *climbs into bed.*

BILLIE *changes into* HARRY.

SCENE XII

Scene change: Room to Underground Atlantis. Music fades.

HONEYSUCKLE *and* HARRY *are seated at monitor. Video begins.*

HARRY: What happens now?

Underground Atlantis light up sharp.

HONEYSUCKLE: Hold on, Big Boy . . .

Computer screen reads insert card. HONEYSUCKLE *runs card along keyboard. Monitor flashes, "Try Again."*

HONEYSUCKLE: Shit! I hate when this happens!

HARRY: What's wrong?

HONEYSUCKLE: Nothing, Harry—just sometimes the card won't read and I've gotta punch in all the numbers by hand.

HONEYSUCKLE *runs the card through again. Monitor flashes, "Approved."*

HONEYSUCKLE: Good! We're in!

HARRY: Now what?

Two figures appear on screen. Crash test dummies. Naked, faceless identities: one man one woman.

HONEYSUCKLE: Tell me what you want, Harry. How about this?

On monitor, the female dummy grabs the male's cock. As the scene progresses, HONEYSUCKLE *reacts to whatever the dummies are doing.* HARRY's *attention is focused on the monitor for the entire session.*

HONEYSUCKLE: Want me to make it bigger? Oooh, Harry! Make it bigger! Make it bigger—Oh, God! It's so big and hard . . . You like it when I do that? Oooh! I want you to fuck me, Harry . . . Fuck me, Harry! Fuck me from behind . . . Ooooh! That's it—Yeah.Push it in me! Oh—Easy, you hurt me! Easy . . . Oooh! Yeah! Like that . . . Slow . . . It's so big! Oh—Hurt me, Yeah! Faster! Faster! Oh, Harry—I'm gonna cum! Harry, You're making me cum! Oh . . . Push—Harder! Harder! Oh! Ooooohhh . . . Harry!

The dummies stand up and face out, then disappear from the monitor.

HARRY: That's it?

HONEYSUCKLE: That's it, Harry. Here's your credit card.

Underground Atlantis light out sharp.

Audio: Jazz music rises.

Exit HONEYSUCKLE.

HARRY *changes back to* BILLIE.

SCENE XIII

Scene change: Underground Atlantis to room. BILLIE *gets into bed and* BLANCHE *lays down on top of him.*

BILLIE: Blanche? Blanche? What's happening?

Low room lights up sharp. BLANCHE *rises to knees on bed above* BILLIE.

BLANCHE: You're not the one that's hard . . .

Pause. BLANCHE *remains motionless—suspending reality.*

BILLIE: That's it . . .

Right hand reaches out for notebook, slithers out from under BLANCHE. *Leans on desk. Opens notebook and writes.*

BILLIE: "He's" not the one that hard. *(Continues writing.)*

Room lights fade.

Exit BLANCHE.

BILLIE *changes into* LATIMER.

SCENE XIV

Scene change: room to cell. Jazz music fades.

LATIMER *stands* CS—*loooking up at Ma.*

LATIMER: Dear Ma . . . *(Cell lights up sharp.)* My writing career is finally taking off. The Post ran my "Good Cooks Come In Small Kitchens" piece, and The Gazette's about to publish "I'm A Prisoner—Aren't We All." So I think this time around I got something to give. *(Blushes.)* You know, the guards voted me most popular con. *(Turns.)* Pretty please Parole Board—Please Please Please! *(Turns out.)* Oughta get paroled—Folks—any day now, and then it'll be the straight and narrow. *(Looks up.)* Hey, Ma—guess what? I'm completely reformed. *(Turns out.)* And, Folks—you know—I owe it all to Indigo. *(Looks up.)* Ma—wish you coulda met her . . . *(Pause.)* But once I'm free . . . Who needs her? *(Turns out.)* Breaks my heart . . . *(Crossing to bunk.)* She's gotta go . . .

LATIMER *sits and writes.*

LATIMER: My Dear, Sweet, Darling— Beloved Indigo: Although you are my cellmate, I cannot take you with me. 'Cause out there . . . *(Pause.)* 'Cause out there—we'd face only disappointment. *(Smirks.)* Nice touch—her words . . . Always, Latimer. *(Pause.)* P.S.—Sorry . . .

(INDIGO enters dressed as hardened con)

INDIGO: There's too much sorrow in the world already.

LATIMER: *(Hides letter.)* Indigo—Hey! Welcome back home.

INDIGO *goes to pull up dress and finds striped convict suit instead—panics; pulls at sleeves in disbelief; grabs crotch and feels a penis.*

LATIMER: How was your day?

INDIGO: *(Removing hand from crotch—accepts new role.)* Prison life's tough, you gutless sack of shit!

LATIMER: Take a deep breath, Hon. Always works for me. *(Pause.)* That's it! Hold it in. Now-Then, let it out slow . . . "-ly." There—Feeling better? *(INDIGO nods.)* Good.

INDIGO: Sorry—I snapped.

LATIMER: Hey—Enough sorrow, right? *(Sits.)* You know—First thing, When we get out . . . I'll buy you a brand-new wardrobe.

Pause. INDIGO *sits; suspicious.*

LATIMER: *(Crossing heart.)* Swear! See? On my dead mother's soul! *(Looks up.)* Hey, Ma! I sweared on your soul . . .

Pause.

INDIGO: Latimer?

LATIMER: Yeah, Baby?

INDIGO: What have you been writing?

LATIMER: *(Eyes letter.)* Well . . . Uhh-love poem, Indigo . . . I've written you a love poem . . . S'posed to be a big surprise . . .

Pause.

INDIGO: Can I read it?

LATIMER: By all means! *(Gives letter to INDIGO.)* But . . . *(Whispers.)* Try to keep an open mind.

Pause. LATIMER *inches away.*

INDIGO: *(Reads out loud.)* My Dear, Sweet, Darling— Beloved Indigo: Although you are my cellmate—I cannot take you with me . . . *(Reads on silently to self.)*

Pause.

LATIMER: Say—Folks, when I'm released—you know . . . I'm due a wad of dough . . . Comes to—18 cents a day.

INDIGO: *(Out loud.)* "Her Words"?

LATIMER: *(Ignoring* INDIGO.*)* Which—granted, Ain't so much . . .

INDIGO: *(Bitterly.)* Thanks?

LATIMER: But Tally up a year's worth, multiplied by 41 . . . *(Quickly.)* And Folks—without a doubt—I'm a shoo-in to get by.

Pause. LATIMER *shuffles feet.*

INDIGO: Sorry?

LATIMER: *(Smiling, to* INDIGO.*)* One for Ma!

INDIGO: Don't get cute, you rat-faced fuck!

LATIMER: *(Forcing smile to remain.)* Ah—Come on! *(Takes back letter.)* Laugh it up, Sweets . . . It was "only" a joke.

INDIGO: Like the time you killed that guard?

LATIMER: I'm "surprised" you still remember.

INDIGO: *(Slipping long knife out from under bunk.)* If you think you can just waltz away and leave me high and dry . . . Well, Buddy, let me tell you—then . . . . you're in for a big surprise! Give me the scratch . . . *(Raising knife.)* Now! Pay up—or else!

LATIMER: *(Kneels—pleading.)* But, Baby—I'm broke!

INDIGO: *(Shoves knife to* LATIMERS'S *throat.)* Don't fuck with me, Smallfry!

LATIMER: *(Squirming.)* Put down the knife!

INDIGO: Then, Fork it over.

LATIMER: What?

INDIGO: The stash you've got sewn up . . . Inside—yourself . . .

Pause.

LATIMER: *(Looks up.)* Hey—you know, Ma—She's right! *(Looks out.* INDIGO *slowly lowers knife.)* Now—We live forever . . . Inside someone else . . .

Long pause. They smile at each other. All is well again.

Cell light off sharp. Music rises. Exit INDIGO.

LATIMER *changes back to* BILLIE.

SCENE XV

Scene change: Cell to room.

Audio: Music continues.

BILLIE *pulls page from typewriter. Room lights slowly rise.*

BILLIE *sits at desk, peering closely at his page. Feeling somewhat self-content, he sets page down softly. Crosses* SL. *Slowly opens door. Peeks out.*

OLD MAN'S VOICE: *(Offstage.)* I seen that girl come out of your room. *(Pause.)* I took her upstairs—with me.

BILLIE *slams the door. Lights and music start to fade. Crossing the stage, he sits on the bed until lights and music are gone.*

THE END

FRONTIER A-GO-GO

A Play (Onwords)

PRODUCTION NOTES:

Frontier A-Go-Go is (and was) a sweet piece of theater, and the last one I staged at The Marilyn. The play involves a strange man living on the Nebraska plains, circa 1872, who uses a time machine to bring two couples back to iron out the wrinkles of the future. Thus:

> *What if the world is too much to bear?*
> *Invent one where it isn't.*

Here . . .

FRONTIER A-GO-GO

A
Play
(Onwords)

MEAN TIME:

(prelude)

STAGE 1:
(pretense)

STAGE 2:
(program)

STAGE 3:
(project)

STAGE 4:
(partners)

STAGE 5:
(premise)

STAGE 6:
(prospect)

STAGE 7:
(progress)

HABITAT:

Nebraska—A Plain; Autumn—1872

HABITUS:

A capsized boat (USR-USC) with hole in hull, fixed up inside as cabin.

A time machine (USC-angled out DSR) off portside stern of boat.

A glowing campfire (DSR to boat entry) with stand supporting pot of beans.

A sawed-off length of railroad tie roosts behind campfire.

A trail (far SL) leads back behind time machine (TM).

*A monitor (built in TM) remains concealed
until handle (inside boat) is pulled—revealing screen.*

Background entifies endless fields.

HABITANT:

JACKSON—*imitation manifest destiny.*

HARDWARE:

A foot-long stick (one end in fire) painted to look hot.

A wooden ladle (half-submerged) protruding from beanpot.

5 wooden bowls in boat (on floor—SR of entry).

A diagram (in boat) of TM microscheme.

An old bucket (in boat).

Half a joint (on DAVON).

FIRST PHASE:
(*Video*)

2 Day Rock Concert—Upstate New York; 1972
(a clearing and trees at the edge of a forest)

RACHAEL: *placid pre-earth mother salting self-inflicted wounds*
DAVON: *ne'er-do-well-meant hap-go-luck*
BILBO: *uptight cool jerk*
PARTRIDGE: *high-strung ditz with tits*

sleeping bag; joint (on PARTRIDGE*)—book of matches (on* BILBO*)*

SECOND PHASE:
(*Video*)

To Your Health Vegetarian Eatery—San Francisco; 1997
(a restaurant with open kitchen and big window facing street)

SABBATH: *self-possessed facade surrounding circumstantial scars*
YEWELL: *clean-cut head on shoulders stretching given inch to mile*
DENTYNE: *prig-perfect waiter*
CHARLIE: *chef compelled to sharpen knives*

2 bottles (oxy-herbal)—limes; 2-menus—phone; a tray—3 knives

THIRD PHASE:
(*Video*)

Little Big Horn; 1876

RACHAEL
SITTING BULL: *a lech*
LITTLE THORN: *a stoic*

automatic pistol; duffel bag—a tree stump

FOURTH PHASE:
(*Video*)

Inventions, Inc. Office—Los Angeles; 1995

YEWELL
MAX *&* MOSHE: *partners in crime*
BILLY MACHARAINA: *dance-crazed client*

TM *microscheme (on* YEWELL*); micro-camera (in desk drawer)*

FIFTH PHASE:
(*Video*)
Same as First Phase

RACHAEL *&* DAVON

sleeping bag

SIXTH PHASE:
(*Video*)
Short Cut To Woodstock; 1969

DAVON
BUSTER *&* WOODCHUCK: *2 logger outdoorsmen*

pick-up truck

(PRELUDE)

Audio: Acoustic guitar strums old pioneer ballads. Sound floats from backstage as if distant.

Onstage: moon, campfire and boat entry light on.

JACKSON *inside boat, holding bucket in place.*

Audio: Acoustic guitar strumming "Polly-Wolly Doodle" begins accompanied by the faint sound of crickets chirping.

Boat entry light fades.

RACHAEL *and* DAVON *(Off* SL.*) in place.*

Auido: Guitar strumming fades; cricket chirps rise.

JACKSON *appears in boat hole with bucket at side. Rears back with bucket to put out the fire.*

Blackout.

Audio: Sound of water dousing a fire. Cricket chirps rise to level of madness.

JACKSON *pulls handle to open* TM *screen.*

Audio: Cricket chirps end abruptly.

STAGE 1:
(pretense)

Campfire, noon and boat entry light up sharp.

JACKSON: *(Inside boat.)* Let's see—Yep, they're finished Now . . . 'at Sabbath got "conceived" . . .

(Video begins.)

Oh-ul—Here goes Nothin' . . . Maybe "this" time. Ahh—Justine . . .

FIRST PHASE:
(Video)*

Two day rock concert—Upstate New York; 1973. Sound of first band (Free Will) warming up continues in background throughout.

SHOT 1: WIDE—EDGE OF FOREST.

Inside a sleeping bag, RACHAEL *and* DAVON *consummate making love between trees. Camera zooms in.*

LEAD SINGER: *(Off-camera.)* Y'all Ready?

Crowd roars.

DAVON *rolls off* RACHAEL *panting.*

RACHAEL: That . . . was . . . the best . . .

DAVON: Yeah . . . How many times we make it?

RACHAEL: Uh . . .

LEAD SINGER: Ok!

RACHAEL: Let's see . . .

LEAD SINGER: You want it? You got it! P.O.W. Dude! (*"P.O.W. Dude" is a psychedelic version of "Polly-Wolly Doodle." Song begins in background.*)

RACHAEL: We met last night while Roach Clip was playing . . .

DAVON: Right.

*All videos play on Time Machine monitor.

SHOT 2: WIDE—OVER RACHAEL AND DAVON

BILBO *and* PARTRIDGE *approach.*

RACHAEL: You asked me for my soul . . .

DAVON: *(Laughs.)* I was really high.

BILBO: Man, You coming?

SHOT 3: TIGHT—DAVON CLIMBING OUT OF SLEEPING BAG

DAVON: Hey! *(Crawls out of sleeping bag.)* Sure. *(Stands.)* Just— *(Turns.)* Let me . . . *(Zips.)*

SHOT 4: MEDIUM—BILBO, PARTRIDGE AND DAVON (WITH BACK TO CAMERA)

BILBO: This is Partridge.

PARTRIDGE: *(Flaps hands.)* Like . . . the bird . . .

DAVON: *(Turns.)* There.

RACHAEL: *(Enters frame.)* Rachael. *(To* PARTRIDGE.*)* He's Davon.

BILBO: *(To* RACHAEL.*)* I'm Bilbo.

SHOT 5: MEDIUM—BILBO AND DAVON

DAVON: Hey, Bilbo-Man? You Got "Anything"?

BILBO: *(Holds out hand.)* Joint Please, Partridge. *(Smiles.)*

SHOT 6: TIGHT—PARTRIDGE FROM CHEST UP

PARTRIDGE: *(Pulls joint out from breasts.)* Open Sesame! *(Hands joint to* BILBO.*)*

Camera follows: BILBO *and* DAVON.

DAVON: Far-out!

BILBO: *(Lights joint.)* Tell you, Man . . . *(Pause. Exhales.)* These are magical days . . . *(Hands joint to* DAVON.*)*

SHOT 7: RACHAEL FROM CHEST UP

RACHAEL: Kent State? Saigon?

SHOT 8: OVER PARTRIDGE'S RIGHT SHOULDER; RACHAEL AND DAVON (WITH JOINT)

PARTRIDGE: *(To* RACHAEL.*)* What do you do?

DAVON: *(Inhaling.)* Nothing like Woodstock.

RACHAEL: Go to school . . .

PARTRIDGE: Me, too . . .

SHOT 9: BILBO, PARTRIDGE AND DAVON

BILBO: You were there?

DAVON: *(Exhaling.)* Pigs hassled me for pot. *(Holds out joint to* RACHAEL—*off camera.)* Want a toke?

PARTRIDGE: My turn . . .

BILBO: Be cool!

SHOT 10: CLOSE UP OF RACHAEL

RACHAEL: *(Takes joint.)* Why not?

SHOT 11: SAME AS SHOT 7

PARTRIDGE: Who's on?

RACHAEL: *(Inhaling.)* Free Will.

DAVON: *(Zonked.)* Wow!

PARTRIDGE: *(Disappointed.)* Oh . . .

DAVON: Good stuff.

SHOT 12: CLOSE UP—BILBO'S FACE

BILBO: Blond 'Nam.

SHOT 13: PARTRIDGE—OVER RACHAEL'S RIGHT SHOULDER

RACHAEL: *(Handing* PARTRIDGE *joint.)* Don't you dig 'em?

PARTRIDGE: *(Inhaling.)* I . . . Just . . . Love Pot!

SHOT 14: SAME AS SHOT 5

RACHAEL: *(Staring at distance.)* Their music speaks the issues.

SHOT 15: LEFT OF PARTRIDGE; PARTRIDGE, BILBO, AND DAVON

DAVON: Seen Peacock?

BILBO: Not lately . . .

PARTRIDGE: *(Still inhaling.)* Man . . .

DAVON: Prob'ly up front.

BILBO: Yeah . . .

Weird hum sound begins.

SHOT 15: SAME AS SHOT 4

BILBO: *(To* PARTRIDGE*)* Hey—You! *(Laughs.)* Gimme that! *(Takes joint.)*

RACHAEL: I feel . . . strange.

DAVON: What's that noise?

PARTRIDGE: Zonk!

SHOT 16: RACHAEL AND DAVON—FULL

BILBO: *(Off-camera—hands* DAVON *joint.)* Here you are, My Man.

Weird hum rises.

PARTRIDGE: *(Off-camera.)* Hey! What's going on?

RACHAEL *and* DAVON *melt.*

Weird hum ends.

SHOT 16: BILBO AND PARTRIDGE

PARTRIDGE: What happened? Where are they?

BILBO: *(Grabs sleeping bag.)* Man, Dude ripped me off!

PARTRIDGE: But . . .

SHOT 17: BILBO WALKING OFF THROUGH FIELD

BILBO: Come on! *(Yells at sky.)* I'll catch you later Davon.

SHOT 18: CLOSE UP—PARTRIDGE (STARING INTO CAMERA)

PARTRIDGE: That . . . was pretty cool.

Screen goes dark—hum begins.

Blackout. Monitor off. Close TM.

JACKSON *sits by fire.* RACHAEL *and* DAVON *stand side by side in front of* TM.

Quick flash of colored beams shoot out from TM.

Campfire, noon and boat entry lights up.

DAVON *puffs unlit joint.*

JACKSON: Want some beans?

RACHAEL: *(Dazed.)* Wow! I'm stoned.

DAVON: *(Stops puffing.)* Hey . . . the joint went out.

RACHAEL: Bummer.

DAVON: *(To* RACHAEL.*)* Got matches?

RACHAEL: Not on me.

JACKSON: Folks Hungry? Dig in.

DAVON: *(To* JACKSON*)* Now that's a "cool" jacket.

JACKSON: There's plenty . . .

RACHAEL: Ask him.

Pause.

DAVON: *(Steps forward.)* Got a light?

JACKSON: *(Holds up stick.)* Use a stick.

DAVON: Huh?

JACKSON: *(Puffs.)* Like this.

DAVON: Oh . . . *(Turns to* RACHAEL*)* Must be a "vision."

RACHAEL: Psychedelic True Grit.

DAVON: Yeah, But that ain't John Wayne.

RACHAEL: No, I think we were dosed.

DAVON: *(Looks up.)* Hey, Bilbo-Man . . . Bless you!

JACKSON: I sent fer Y'all Both.

Pause.

RACHAEL: Who are you?

JACKSON: Name's Jackson.

DAVON: Why both? I mean, Why not just kidnap some chick for yourself?

JACKSON: Ul—

RACHAEL: *(Pissed.)* What's wrong with Me?

JACKSON: Cuz—

DAVON: *(Nuzzles* RACHAEL.*)* I found you First!

RACHAEL: *(Breaks away.)* Oh?

JACKSON: Plan, calls for 2's.

RACHAEL: *(To* JACKSON.*)* Then I'm stuck with "this" Jerk?

DAVON: Say What! Who's a Jerk?

RACHAEL: I ain't "something" you found!

DAVON: Aww!

RACHAEL: Kidnap some chick?

DAVON: I was messin' around.

RACHAEL: So . . . *(Squats.)* Jackson—How goes it?

JACKSON: *(Pokes fire with stick.)* Just fine Rachael, thanks . . .

DAVON: *(Unhinges.)* You "know"—uhh . . . He knows you?

RACHAEL: *(To* JACKSON, *of* DAVON'S *name.)* What's His?

JACKSON: *(Holds out stick to* DAVON.*)* Want the stick?

Pause.

DAVON: *(Looks at joint.)* Uhh . . . *(Looks at* RACHAEL.*)*

RACHAEL: I'm cool.

DAVON: Oh . . . *(Pockets joint.)*

RACHAEL: One hit did the trick. *(Quickly to* JACKSON.*)* Well?

DAVON: *(Spills.)* It's David.

RACHAEL: What's David?

DAVON: My name. David Aaron.

RACHAEL: Who's Davon?

DAVON: The Ideal!

RACHAEL: All Lies covet Change.

DAVON: Come on!

RACHAEL: That's a fact, Jack. *(To* JACKSON.*)* Agree?

JACKSON: Reckon so . . .

DAVON: But!

JACKSON: *(To* DAVON.*)* With what She said—

RACHAEL: *(To* DAVON.*)* See!

JACKSON: *(To* RACHAEL.*)* Not what He done . . .

RACHAEL: *(Smart-assed.)* Shucks.

DAVON: Hey, one night on acid I heard David ask Aaron, "What can We be?" . . . and the answer was Davon.

RACHAEL: *(Leans up to* JACKSON.*)* So Tell, Mr. Wizard—What town was I born?

JACKSON: Larchmont.

DAVON: *(To* RACHAEL.*)* I'm Peekskill!

RACHAEL: No?

DAVON: Straight! You know Red?

JACKSON: 22 years a'fore—

RACHAEL: Who?

JACKSON: 99 on ahead—

DAVON: Red!

RACHAEL: Red—Who?

DAVON: What?

RACHAEL: His "last" name?

DAVON: Wore black . . .

RACHAEL: *(Turns to* JACKSON.*)* Am I braindead, too?

JACKSON: Nope—Just borrowed.

DAVON: Dealt hash.

RACHAEL: Oh, "that" Red!

DAVON: *(Draws on own face.)* Long sideburns . . .

RACHAEL: Yeah!

DAVON: *(Draws again.)* Curly Moustache.

RACHAEL: Small world after all.

DAVON: Like they say— *(Struts.)* It's a Gasssss!

JACKSON: You Folks Want some beans?

RACHAEL: What kind?

JACKSON: Ones I cooked.

DAVON: Man, Who are you Really?

RACHAEL: *(Peeks in boat.)* You mind?

JACKSON: Have a look.

RACHAEL: *(Enters boat.)* Hm . . .

JACKSON: *(To* DAVON.*)* See, That there behind ya's a Time implement.

Pause.

DAVON *turns and stares.*

JACKSON: Found it right here . . . Along my journey West.

DAVON: Implement?

JACKSON: Time Machine.

DAVON: Solid!

RACHAEL: *(Peeks out hole.)* Why Us?

JACKSON: I'm gettin' to that part.

DAVON: Our Own Magic Bus!

RACHAEL: *(Exits boat.)* So What's with the Boat?

DAVON: Yeah, is that like an "Ark"? *(*RACHEL *glares.)* He Said he needs 2's.

JACKSON: 'n-You'll "do" . . . fer' a Start.

DAVON: *(Worried.)* uh-Do?

RACHAEL: Do What?

DAVON: I Ain't fixing no Boat!

RACHAEL: I'm coming "undone"!

DAVON: Can't collect if I "work"!

JACKSON: This here ain't no "job." Simmer Down—Have some grub.

RACHAEL: Where are we?

JACKSON: Nebraska.

DAVON: *(Boasts.)* I Thumbed through there Once.

RACHAEL: Nebraska?

JACKSON: Earned statehood 'bout 5 years ago . . .

DAVON: Same year I hitched out to California! Crashed at Big Sur in some pad made of mud . . . Then booked to Frisco for The Summer of Love.

RACHAEL: *(To DAVON.)* Will you Can the Flashbacks! *(To JACKSON.)* Man, What's today's Date?

JACKSON: October 11th.

DAVON: No sweat. It's the same.

RACHAEL: *(To DAVON.)* Yeah right. *(To JACKSON.)* But what "year"?

DAVON: '67, In June.

RACHAEL: Not Then you Fool—Now!

JACKSON: 1872.

RACHAEL *and* DAVON *still-pause.*

RACHAEL: *(To JACKSON.)* 18-?

DAVON: Don't wig—

JACKSON: Yep!

DAVON: To Everything "turn."

JACKSON: Back one hundred years Now, from where Y'all just were.

DAVON: *(Flips.)* The Concert! Free Will! Man—Condition's up Next!

RACHAEL: Yeah, Next "century."

JACKSON: Time t' Dwell 'n the Past!

DAVON: That's Really a Drag. They're one Dynamite band.

RACHAEL: *(To* DAVON.*)* We're bound to come down, Right?

DAVON: So?

RACHAEL: Deal with it "then."

DAVON: Yeah, well, I guess. *(To* RACHAEL.*)* You know—You're pretty cool.

RACHAEL: *(To* JACKSON.*)* Okay. Spill the beans.

JACKSON: Want some Beans? Grab a bowl.

RACHAEL: *(Slaps knee with contempt.)* Yah-Hoo!

DAVON: Man, I'm Thirsty! *(To* JACKSON.*)* Got something to Drink?

JACKSON: *(To self.)* Water drum's 'bout empty.

RACHAEL: *(To* JACKSON.*)* So's stacking the deck!

JACKSON: *(To self.)* ul-River's not far . . .

DAVON: *(Snaps.)* I got an Idea! *(Turns to* TM.*)* Just crank up this baby 'n Send for some Beer!

JACKSON: *(To self.)* Been puttin' it off.

DAVON: *(Feebly searching pockets.)* Let me foot the bill.

RACHAEL: *(To* DAVON.*)* Thought you were tapped?

DAVON: *(Winces.)* Heh!

JACKSON: *(To self.)* Take 3 trips t' fill.

DAVON: *(Mr. Humble.)* Say, Jack, Look I'm short, man—uhh . . . Next Launch, I Pay!

JACKSON: *(To DAVON.)* Can't be done.

DAVON: Why?

JACKSON: Son, Whatever man made . . . got no place in time, a'fore it's created . . .

Pause.

DAVON: *(To RACHAEL.)* Sounds heavy, Huh?

RACHAEL: *(To DAVON.)* Then Why the "machine"?

DAVON: *(To JACKSON.)* Man, She's got a point . . . How'd That make the scene?

Pause.

JACKSON *stirs beans.*

RACHAEL: Alright! It's Nebraska. He's David, Sky's Blue. So lay off them beans Jack, and cop to the Truth.

JACKSON: *(To DAVON.)* Cop to?

RACHAEL: Come Clean!

DAVON: She means, Cut to the Chase.

JACKSON: *(To RACHAEL.)* Uh, Chase?

RACHAEL: She means Now!

JACKSON: Oh, Well—First off . . . She's Pregnant.

Pause.

RACHAEL *stares* DAVON *down.*

RACHAEL: Smooth move, Ex-Lax!

DAVON: Huh?

RACHAEL: Thought you pulled out?

DAVON: I Did!

JACKSON: Not that "last" time.

DAVON: Oh . . .

JACKSON: It's a girl.

RACHAEL: Ha! No doubt.

DAVON: *(Snuggles up to* RACHAEL.*)* We're having a baby! *(To* JACKSON.*)* Right? *(*JACKSON *nods.)* When we get back?

JACKSON: Ya'll could have her here, but ain't much sense t' that.

RACHAEL: You Say, There's a "river"?

JACKSON: *(Points* USL.*)* Yep, down 'long that trail . . . Flat as a shingle, all quiet 'n "still."

RACHAEL: *(To* DAVON.*)* Go for a walk?

DAVON: Sure, uh . . . *(To* JACKSON.*)* How much time we got?

JACKSON: 'Bout Oh, Say enough to pursue what you want.

Pause.

DAVON: Far out!

RACHAEL: Right on!

DAVON: *(Poses.)* Let's Boogie! *(Turns head to* JACKSON.*)* Ciao, Jack.

RACHAEL: *(Turns head to* JACKSON.*)* You sure "He's" the father?

DAVON: *(Uptight.)* Hey! Cut me some slack!

JACKSON: Done hurt the boy's feelin's . . .

RACHAEL: *(Teasing playful, pokes* DAVON'S *shoulder.)* Aww . . .

JACKSON: He ain't All that bad.

DAVON: Could do a lot worse!

RACHAEL: *(Hugging* DAVON *from behind.)* Hey, loosen up . . . "Dad."

DAVON: After You, Foxy Mama . . . We're splitting, My Man . . . Uh-Which way's the river?

JACKSON: *(Points* USL.*)* Just follow that path.

RACHAEL: *(Tugs* DAVON'S *arm.)* We could . . . *(Shimmies.)* Skinny-dip!

DAVON: *(Checks* JACKSON.*)* Well?

JACKSON: *(Shrugs.)* Durn good idea! Indian summer's the best time 'a year.

RACHAEL: *(Pulling* DAVON'S *arm.)* Come on!

DAVON: *(Pulls arm back.)* Rachael, Wait! *(To* JACKSON.*)* You mean "real" Indians?

RACHAEL *eyes* TM.

JACKSON: No different than us.

RACHAEL: *(Plots to self.)* But with this—they can win . . .

JACKSON: *(Concerned.)* Now Folks, heh. Don't worry. It's safe a-fore Dark . . .

DAVON: *(To* RACHAEL.*)* You like the name Sabbath?

RACHAEL: *(Grabbing* DAVON's *arm.)* Jack—Later!

DAVON *waves to* JACKSON.

RACHAEL: *(To* DAVON.) We'll talk.

RACHAEL *and* DAVON *exit down trail* USL.

JACKSON: I'll save y'all some beans.

Noonlight starts to fade.

Conversation trails off.

RACHAEL: Where'd you get Sabbath?

DAVON: My favorite group.

RACHAEL: Thought you said Condition?

DAVON: Well . . .

Pause. Lights fade.

JACKSON: Time for Stage 2.

Blackout.

JACKSON *enters boat.*

Video begins in blackout with song ("Powa Doo").

End Stage 1.

STAGE 2:
(program)

JACKSON *(inside boat) opens* TM *screen.*

Video continues (black) with music.

Campfire, noon and boat entry lights up.

JACKSON: Let's see—San Francisco, 1997 . . . And then To Your Health, Vegetarian Restaurant . . .

SECOND PHASE:
(Video)

Music continues.

SHOT 1. THROUGH WINDOW OF RESTAURANT: TO YOUR HEALTH

SABBATH *(in profile) stands* SR *to front door waiting on sidewalk for* YEWELL, *her date. Her face seems content to soak in her surroundings but one second later looks full of regret.*

> *Street traffic fades to level sound from inside restaurant where audio of song called "Powa-Doo" blends softly into background. "Powa-Doo" is a new-age rendition of "Polly-Wolly Doodle."*

YEWELL *appears with a smile.*

SABBATH *smiles back taking one half-step toward him and puts out both hands almost wanting a kiss.*

Thrown by this, YEWELL *stops three feet away.*

DENTYNE: *(Off-camera.)* Maybe . . .

YEWELL *shakes* SABBATH'S *hand.*

DENTYNE: *(Same.)* Maybe . . .

Camera angle widens to include waiter DENTYNE *who's profile fills right side of screen.*

DENTYNE: Hey, Charlie?

YEWELL *points at the door.* SABBATH *nods.*

CHARLIE: *(Sharpening knife in kitchen.)* Yeahhh?

SABBATH *and* YEWELL *head to door.*

Camera widens showing phone in front of DENTYNE.

DENTYNE: *(Turns head slowly to camera.)* I think . . . *(Picks up phone.)* They're coming in.

YEWELL *opens door.*

SHOT 2. HOST STATION OF RESTAURANT

DENTYNE *on phone at host station, surrounded by empty tables.* SABBATH *and* YEWELL *enter and stand next to station.* SABBATH *looks around.* YEWELL *stares at* DENTYNE.

DENTYNE: *(Wings it.)* Gleason, you say? *(Writes name in book.)* Uhh . . . Party of seven? Yes.

YEWELL: Table for two.

DENTYNE: Uh . . . *(Holds up finger.)* Right with you—Yes! *(Writes.)* 8:30—P . . . *(Dots period.)* M . . . *(Dots period. Faintly, phone emits disconnected number sound.)* Uh . . . Thanks—You're all set! *(Quickly hangs up.)*

YEWELL *snickers.*

SABBATH: *(To* YEWELL.*)* What?

DENTYNE: Table for Dos?

YEWELL: *(Smart-assed.)* Sí!

SABBATH: *(To* YEWELL.*)* Why are you laughing?

SHOT 3: SL DENTYNE—FULL PROFILE (GRABBING MENUS)

DENTYNE: *(Looks around.)* There! A nice window seat. Follow me. *(Leaves frame.* SABBATH *and* YEWELL *stay put.)* Something wrong?

SHOT 4: OVER YEWELL'S LEFT SHOULDER; SABBATH AND YEWELL

SABBATH: People watch when I eat.

YEWELL: *(To* DENTYNE.*)* We'd like another table, Sport.

SHOT 5: SAME AS SHOT 3

DENTYNE: *(Off camera.)* How 'bout . . . *(Crosses* SL—*leaves frame.)* This one over here?

SHOT 6: CLOSE UP—SABBATH AND YEWELL

YEWELL: *(To* SABBATH.*)* Up to You?

SABBATH: Okay!

YEWELL: *(To* DENTYNE.*)* Sold!

SHOT 7: DENTYNE STANDING SR TO TABLE WITH MENUS

DENTYNE: I'm Dentyne, Your Waiter.

SHOT 8: SABBATH AND YEWELL SNICKER

SHOT 9: SAME AS SHOT 7

DENTYNE: Any preference of "seats"?

SABBATH *and* YEWELL *enter frame (*SR *foreground).*

SABBATH: *(To* YEWELL.*)* Like, I want that one! *(Points at far* SL *chair).*

YEWELL: *(Crossing to chair.)* Madam . . . *(Pulls chair out.)* Allow Me!

SABBATH *sits—*YEWELL *crosses* SR *sits.*

SHOT 10: SL—SABBATH AND YEWELL AT TABLE

DENTYNE: *(Enters frame. Snidely.)* First date?

SABBATH: *(To* YEWELL.*)* How'd He know?

DENTYNE: *(Holds out menus.)* To Your Health . . .

YEWELL: *(Grabs menu.)* To your "tip"!

SHOT 11: CLOSE-UP OF DENTYNE

DENTYNE: Our Special Today is Cabbage En Croute. And, Might I suggest . . . An Oxy-Herbal Spring water?

SHOT 12: SR—SABBATH AND YEWELL AT TABLE

SABBATH: *(To* DENTYNE.*)* What is this music?

YEWELL: *(Looks up at* DENTYNE.*)* Check the disc, Sport!

SHOT 13: PROFILE OF DENTYNE FROM WAIST UP

DENTYNE *turns toward kitchen.*

YEWELL: *(Off camera.)* And Bring two Oxy-Herbals.

DENTYNE *leaves frame.*

YEWELL: *(Off camera.)* What?

SHOT 14: SABBATH AND YEWELL AT TABLE—SABBATH POINTS AT MENU

YEWELL: And . . . one Tofu Board.

SHOT 15: CHARLIE IN KITCHEN. DENTYNE ENTERS FRAME

DENTYNE: *(Sticking ticket on spike.)* One Tofu Board.

CHARLIE: *(Staring at knife blade.)* On the fire!

SHOT 16: SAME AS SHOT 7

YEWELL: *(Laughs.)* Dentyne?

SABBATH *laughs.*

SHOT 17: SAME AS SHOT 14

DENTYNE: *(Looks* SR—*sneers.)* Use up the stuff that expired last week. *(Leaves frame.* CHARLIE *sharpens knife some more.)*

SHOT 18: SABBATH AND YEWELL FRONT AND CENTER AT TABLE

SABBATH: So, How long have you worked on the 7th floor?

YEWELL: Oh, Maybe two months.

SABBATH: I've been there almost four!

YEWELL: Stylin' computers!

SABBATH: You like it?

YEWELL: Pays rent.

SABBATH: Yeah, I've got three roommates.

YEWELL: *(Drifts.)* Some day, I'll be rich . . .

DENTYNE *enters frame carrying tray with 2 bottled waters, 2 glasses with ice, and 2 lime wedges on separate napkins.*

YEWELL: So, What's up with Sabbath?

SABBATH: My dad's favorite band.

DENTYNE: *(Sets down glasses.)* Two Oxy-Herbals. *(To* YEWELL*)* Lime? *(*YEWELL *glares. Offers lime to* SABBATH*.)*

SABBATH: *(Shakes head.)* No Thanks.

DENTYNE *pours* SABBATH'S *water.*

YEWELL: *(Grabs bottle from* DENTYNE'S *hand.)* I'll Pour!

YEWELL *fills* SABBATH'S *glass—then his own.*

Weird hum begins.

SHOT 19: CLOSE UP—DENTYNE; PROFILE

DENTYNE: The Disc is by Language. The Track's Powa-Doo.

SHOT 20: SABBATH AND YEWELL—FULL; WIDE ANGLE AT TABLE—BOTH SIPPING WATER

YEWELL: What's that noise?

SABBATH: I feel strange!

DENTYNE: *(Off camera.)* So, Have you decided?

SABBATH *and* YEWELL *dissolve in time*

Weird hum ends.

SHOT 21: SL—DENTYNE'S BACK AND EMPTY TABLE

DENTYNE: *(Turns to kitchen.)* Hey, Charlie?

CHARLIE: *(Off camera.)* Yeah . . .

DENTYNE: um-I think you better . . . 86 the-uh tofu board.

Blackout. Monitor off. Close TM.

Weird hum continues.

SABBATH (SR) *and* YEWELL(SL) *sit facing one another in front of* TM.

JACKSON *sits in same place by fire.*

Colored beams shoot from machine.

Campfire, noon and boat entry lights up.

JACKSON: Y'all want some Beans?

YEWELL: *(Oblivious.)* I'll have Cabbage En Croute . . . *(To* SABBATH.*)* You Ready to order?

SABBATH: *(To* YEWELL.*)* Like Who is "that" dude?

JACKSON: Name's Jackson . . .

SABBATH: *(To* JACKSON.*)* I'm Sabbath. *(Points.)* He's Yewell.

JACKSON: That so?

YEWELL: Could you locate "our" waiter?

JACKSON: Mighty long way to go.

SABBATH: Well, One thing's for sure . . . This is not To Your Health!

YEWELL: *(Folds arms.)* uh-May I have a word with your "ex" manager?

JACKSON: Now, Son—Settle down . . .

YEWELL: *(Looks around.)* Where's that dickhead, Dentyne?

JACKSON: Ain't conceived as 'a yet.

SABBATH: Prob'ly excess Caffeine!

YEWELL: *(Turns to* SABBATH *with disbelief.)* Huh?

SABBATH: In some bottled waters. It's called Toxic Psychosis, on Caffeine TP dot com—this-uh WebSite I access.

YEWELL: *(To* SABBATH.*)* A-O-L?

SABBATH: Not even, Dude! Except to study French.

YEWELL: Explorer?

SABBATH: I'm on NetScape.

YEWELL: Really—Me Too!

SABBATH: That's so Fresh!

Pause.

SABBATH *blushes.* YEWELL *gloats.*

JACKSON: Yewell here's from Phoenix.

SABBATH: *(To* YEWELL.*)* Cool! I come from New York. My Dad still lives in Peekskill.

JACKSON: *(Softly.)* Her mom died, givin' birth.

SABBATH: *(To* JACKSON.*)* How'd you know? Who told you? Was It Thalia, my Roommate?

JACKSON: Just helpin' break the ice, seeing how it's y'all's "first" date.

SABBATH: *(To* YEWELL.*)* What'd you E-mail Half the planet?

YEWELL: Hardly.

SABBATH: Who Else knew?

JACKSON: Peaceful place . . .

SABBATH: Look! If you're some Pirate Hacker Dude, Get Off our Data-Base!

JACKSON: Young lady, Ain't no pirate! I just "borrowed" y'all a stretch.

SABBATH: Like, for some new CD Rom—you know, Premarket Beta-Test?

JACKSON: um-No, This here's Nebraska—

YEWELL: *(To* SABATTH.*)* Boring Graphics. Title's Lame . . .

SABBATH: But He's Hella Inter-Active!

YEWELL: How 'bout, *Homeboy on the Range?*

JACKSON: Well down the road those things to come'll happen soon enough. So, While 'yer Here—Enjoy the Past . . .

SABBATH: Say, Why'd you pick on Us?

JACKSON: Kinda hard to explain.

YEWELL: If Not "hard" to believe?

SABBATH: *(To* YEWELL.*)* Chill-out for a sec!

YEWELL: Well, Excuse my Caffeine!

JACKSON: See that there behind you's a Time implement.

SABBATH: You mean like, Way "real"?

JACKSON: The McCoy!

YEWELL: Like, Jack-shit!

JACKSON: Plumb reckon 'bout time you dismount 'yer high horse, Son . . . Cause what lies ahead now, sure needs 'yer support.

YEWELL: *(Schemes inward.)* Hmm—Power . . . Leverage.

JACKSON: *(To appease* SABBATH.*)* Uh-Depends on y'awl both!

SABBATH: Oh?

YEWELL: *(To* SABBATH.*)* Hey, Watch him Sweat.

SABBATH: *(To* YEWELL.*)* Huh?

YEWELL: *(Clasps hands.)* Let's discuss Percs.

JACKSON: Wha?

YEWELL: Percs. You know, Gravy?

JACKSON: uh-Got sauce on them beans!

SABBATH: Like, Do you provide Dental?

JACKSON: Blade'a straw keeps mine clean.

YEWELL: What's our commute like?

JACKSON: Son, As of today . . . That world you lived in's a-hundred 25 years away.

YEWELL: *(Computes.)* Let's see—Ninety seven, uh . . .

SABBATH: Time Sure flies, dude!

YEWELL: Subtract 125—1872.

JACKSON: Boy's Quick with figures!

YEWELL: My first love was Math.

JACKSON: We All got our Passions.

SABBATH: What're You good at Jack?

YEWELL: Cooking beans. Chewing straw. *(Eyes boat.)* Um, Tweakin' out boats. Mighty slim pickins.

SABBATH: Can you do tricks with rope?

JACKSON: Nope! And the boat had a hole 'Fore I showed up . . .

YEWELL: *(Points to* TM.*)* In This?

JACKSON: Naw. That was here, too . . .

SABBATH: You Mean, You just found it? Like, Play Lotto, Dude!

JACKSON: uh-Reckon I might, if I knew what it was.

YEWELL: Then Jack, Send Me back for the winning numbers!

JACKSON: Can't be done!

YEWELL: Why?

JACKSON: Son, Whatever man Made . . . Got no place in time, 'till it's been Created.

YEWELL: Say-ah—If you don't "mind"—let me look at the specs. uh-There's No MicroScheme that I can't circumvent.

JACKSON: Dadburned, uh-done Told 'ya—no if ands or but! All Past binds uh Future By leavin' its Dust.

YEWELL: *(Eyes machine.)* Hmm . . . uh-Speaking of "Time" . . . Could you beam me back to 1849?

SABBATH: *(To* YEWELL.*)* What's up?

YEWELL: *(Whispers to* SABBATH.*)* The Gold Rush!

JACKSON: Son, What's on 'yer mind?

YEWELL: I grab a few Nuggets. We Split-up the find.

JACKSON: *(Shakes head.)* In One out t' other Boy . . . Landsakes alive! Dang sure Got 'yer heart Set uh playing Both sides.

YEWELL: *(Shrugs.)* Hey, When in Rome?

SABBATH: Our-My-Class went junior year! At least those who could "afford" it . . . We drank red wine from a Tree!

JACKSON: Well My, fancy That! Slew a kids 'bove ground . . . Hoo-Lord only knows . . . How'd yuh Ever climb down?

SABBATH: Down?

JACKSON: From at Tree?

SABBATH: No — See, the Tree was Full of wine.

JACKSON: Hm, Learn some'n ev'r day.

YEWELL: I thought Grapes grew on vines.

SABBATH: When our bus stopped for gas near this town west of Rome, These Kids ran by us laughing wrapped in plastic head to toe.

JACKSON: Must 'a been mighty poor . . .

SABBATH: They had Clothes on underneath!

YEWELL: Hey! Sex-Ed's so advanced there, they practice "safe" friendship!

SABBATH: Outside the shop, an old man watched with eyes that fought the sun. He stood and yelled at them to wait, then motioned us to come. So Me 'n Kira followed them . . . Ms. Bynum blew her top. The children swirled around him teasing catch us if you can, Yet up ahead we knew he held the last laugh in his hands.

YEWELL: *(To* JACKSON.*)* Captain! *(Jerks head at* TM.*)* Forward! 20 Minutes, uh . . . 'Ternally Obliged . . .

SABBATH: There, along the ridge above a stream that mirrored clouds
. . . The old man turned his vineyard into magic stomping
grounds. "Look!" he spoke in English, pointing. "Tree you Big
Surprise!" Though "Tree" was just this sawed-off trunk, It had
like "pegs" to climb . . . And near the base, a Spout from which
the old man poured us wine.

JACKSON: uh-Be glad, t' scratch 'yer—back, son . . . when 'yer done
with scratchin' "mine".

SABBATH: When all the pails of grapes they hauled were relayed up
treetop . . . He paired them off between three ropes and rigged
each waist a knot. Those drawn by lot remained below, while half
submerged inside . . . As one crew heaved, the other hoed . . .
compressing Pulp full-stride . . . *(Pause.)*

From where we sat, Time seemed to stop . . . Then tit for tat,
They duly swapped . . .

Pause.

JACKSON: Quite a tale.

YEWELL: You Mean Set-Up!

JACKSON: How, Son?

YEWELL: He got something for Nothing.

SABBATH: The Children had fun.

JACKSON: See Now, They was Happy!

SABBATH: All covered in red.

YEWELL: All "happiness" needs is low Overhead.

JACKSON: hm-Well, I reckon you-uh "got" sump'in there.

YEWELL: I majored in Business.

SABBATH: With ego to spare.

JACKSON: ul-Each Day turns a profit oh-ah, Somewhere's down the line. For All we done earns interest from those riches kept in mind.

SABBATH: *(Rises.)* I, uh—

YEWELL: —What?

SABBATH: I have to . . . *(Blushes.)* Pee. *(Squirms.)* Like—Bad!

YEWELL: Okay. Alright. Say, Jack . . . Where's the Can?

JACKSON: Just go squat between 'em Weeds . . .

SABBATH: What about . . . You know— . . . B-M?

YEWELL: B-M?

SABBATH: Bowel movement. It's a morph for Number 2 . . . I used to work with "special" kids, part time after school.

JACKSON: Well, one 'r two—Pick any spot.

YEWELL: To wipe your Ass—Use either sock!

RACHAEL *and* DAVON'S *playful banter draws near from* USL.

RACHAEL: *(Offstage.)* Fraidy Cat!

DAVON: *(Offstage.)* Not Me!

SABBATH: Who's that?

JACKSON: You'll see.

RACHAEL: *(Appears on trail; stops. Turns back to* DAVON.*)* The Water's . . . *(Sticks left foot out.)* —cold!

DAVON: *(Appears next to* RACHAEL.*)* So? *(Laughs.)* Mark Spitz I ain't. *(Passes* RACHAEL.*)*

RACHAEL: Ha! *(Follows* DAVON.*)* What about the "Buffaloes"?

DAVON: *(Crossing* SR.*)* Come on, They could'a . . .

RACHAEL: *(Stopping* DSL *to* SABBATH.*)* Paranoia!

DAVON: *(Passes* RACHAEL.*)* Started a Stampede!

SABBATH *can't believe her eyes.*

JACKSON: Welcome back!

SABBATH: *(To* DAVON.*)* Dad?

DAVON: *(Waves.)* Howdy, Jack!

SABBATH: *(To* RACHAEL.*)* m-m Mother?

RACHAEL: *(Stares at* SABBATH.*)* Man . . . *(Turns to* JACKSON.*)* Who's She?

Pause. All stare at JACKSON.

JACKSON: *(Level-headed.)* Rachael, Davon . . . Yewell, Sabbath.

SABBATH: *(To* RACHAEL *and* DAVON.*)* I'm your daughter . . . *(Smiles; turns to* YEWELL.*)* They're my parents!

YEWELL: *(To* SABBATH.*)* But I thought, she—

JACKSON: Not just yet!

SABBATH: Like, sorry mom . . .

RACHAEL: For what?

SABBATH: Your death.

Blackout.

Audio: "Polly-Wolly Doodle" begins with just acoustic, then "Powa Doo" fuses in.

End Stage 2.

STAGE 3:
(project)

While music plays, DAVON *crosses stage and stands* SR *to* JACKSON.
RACHAEL *crouches* SL *next to fire.* SABBATH *stands* CS *right behind*
RACHAEL. YEWELL *and* JACKSON *stay put.*

Music slowly fades.

Campfire, noon and boat entry lights up sharp.

RACHAEL: *(To* JACKSON.*)* It isn't Fair!

DAVON: *(Aside.)* I mean, like Wow!

JACKSON: Ain't much tad 'is.

SABBATH: *(To* RACHAEL.*)* You're here right now!

RACHAEL: *(To* SABBATH.*)* But in 9 months, I'm gonna Die!

DAVON: *(To* JACKSON.*)* Man, I'm so bummed I Lost my High!

JACKSON: wha-Least y'all got 'tis Little spell . . . t' Make up fer What
never Was.

RACHAEL: *(Leans in to* JACKSON.*)* Tell me Straight, All shit Aside.
(Of DAVON.*)* Did He name her Sabbath After I died?

JACKSON: uh'd-Say at the time You's leanin' t'ward Jude.

YEWELL: But Sabbath's "unique."

DAVON: *(To* RACHAEL.*)* Told ya'! *(To* JACKSON.*)* What's his name?

JACKSON: Yewell.

DAVON: Yewell? *(Looks at* YEWELL.*)* Hm . . . *(Assumes authority.)* I'm —
Mister Davenport.

YEWELL: *(Dripping sap.)* I've heard Nice things about you Sir.

SABBATH: We met last week at work.

DAVON: Oh? I-uh, See . . . What kine'a "gig" you got?

YEWELL: Well, I "pose" among the "masses." But, Really I'm in charge.

SABBATH: What?

JACKSON: Boy's sure Ambitious.

YEWELL: Helps Me "weed" the slackers Out.

SABBATH: *(To* YEWELL.*)* So-uh, You're like Undercover?

YEWELL: *(To* SABBATH.*)* Don't expose me.

DAVON: *(To* RACHAEL.*)* s'Dude's a Narc!

RACHAEL: Man, Who gives a shit! Let 'm turn in my corpse . . .

YEWELL: uh-Say, Mister "D"? *(Gravely clenches hands.)* My Regards for
your Loss . . .

RACHAEL: Jack, couldn't this turd "maybe" Die in my place?

DAVON: *(To* JACKSON.*)* I'd be Down for that!

SABBATH: *(To* YEWELL.*)* Hey! Our first and last Date!

YEWELL: Look, I'm "sure" We can find uh, Some Alternative?

JACKSON: Can't Nobody 'spire in some others stead.

DAVON: Like Wow! I just realized, man. Sabbath times two. *(Turns
to* SABBATH.*)* She's standing right here . . . *(Turns to* RACHAEL.*)*
'n She's there in your Womb!

SABBATH: *(Bending to* RACHAEL'S *waist. Waves.)* Hi Me!

YEWELL: *(To* DAVON.*)* A Goldmine!

SABBATH: Mom, Hella cool pants!

DAVON: *(To* YEWELL.*)* Say What?

JACKSON: *(To* DAVON.*)* Son—

RACHAEL: *(To* SABBATH.*)* You "like" 'em?

SABBATH: *(Nods head.)* Yeah!

JACKSON: Don't listen!

SABBATH: They're Fresh!

YEWELL: *(To* DAVON.*)* Sir—Would you not Pay to attend your own Birth?

RACHAEL: *(To* SABBATH.*)* Then bite off the cord 'n I'll toss in the shirt!

JACKSON: Say look, if You folks weren't so Give 'n t' Take . . . H'd be more a Hoot since et's Both y'alls first date.

SABBATH: *(To* YEWELL.*)* They met at a Concert!

YEWELL: How very Romantic.

RACHAEL: You "charge" by the pound?

DAVON: I seen Dylan 'n Hendrix!

RACHAEL: *(To* JACKSON.*)* What year're they from?

JACKSON: 1997.

DAVON: *(To* YEWELL.*)* We're '72—

SABBATH: *(Raising hand.)* Um . . . I've got a question.

JACKSON: 'Kay.

SABBATH: How old's my mom?

JACKSON: Oh, uh—

RACHAEL: I'm 22.

SABBATH: But, like—I'm 24.

DAVON: *(To RACHAEL.)* Hey, She's older than You!

RACHAEL: *(To DAVON.)* Man—Who you kidding, You're "just" 23!

YEWELL: *(To DAVON.)* When's your Birthday?

DAVON: *(To YEWELL.)* March 4.

YEWELL: Got you beat by a week . . . Sir—Almost, not Quite. I was born Leap Year Day.

RACHAEL: Lucky world.

DAVON: What a Drag!

YEWELL: No, I made my folks Pay.

SABBATH: Mom, Yours is May 14th.

RACHAEL: Was.

JACKSON: *(To DAVON.)* Son, He most Surely did.

SABBATH: See, Every year I celebrate by eating one fresh fig.

YEWELL: *(To DAVON.)* Eleven!

RACHAEL: Why a "fig"?

SABBATH: They-uh Bloom before their leaves.

JACKSON: *(To DAVON.)* uh-29th ah Ev'ry month, them non-leap years b'tween . . .

RACHAEL: Wow!

DAVON: *(To JACKSON.)* You mean—

YEWELL: *(To* DAVON.*)* Each month!

RACHAEL: That's "deep."

YEWELL: *(Stately.)* They held a party for me.

RACHAEL: *(To* SABBATH.*)* To you, I'm but a figment.

Pause.

DAVON: *(To* YEWELL.*)* Pretty slick—

JACKSON: *(To* DAVON.*)* Nope. Greedy, Son.

YEWELL: *(To* JACKSON.*)* Hey! Leap Years I Agreed to One.

RACHAEL: Alright—Enough! From That to this! Jack, What's your plan?

JACKSON: Ist' Hit 'r miss.

YEWELL: Well Dude, We Claim that Don't mean Squat!

RACHAEL: *(To* YEWELL.*)* Who made you king?

YEWELL: I'm oldest.

SABBATH: Not!

DAVON: *(To* YEWELL.*)* Yeah, She—My daughter—

RACHAEL: *(To* DAVON.*)* Ours!

SABBATH: *(To* YEWELL.*)* I'm older!

JACKSON: Folks, now—

YEWELL: Look Group . . . *(Points to* JACKSON.*)* He's the Poseur!

Pause. All eyes turn to JACKSON.

JACKSON: heh-Must admit Ain't told Y'all much. Cause most 'r time's Been squandered Such.

RACHAEL: That's clever shit. Psych 101. Diverting Focus somewhere else!

SABBATH: *(To* RACHAEL.*)* Professor Thumphy?

RACHAEL: *(To* JACKSON *of* SABBATH.*)* Psychic, Too?

SABBATH: I went to Hartwick, Same as You!

JACKSON: ah's Hopin' y'all uh'd, have 'is Chance.

DAVON: *(To* JACKSON.*)* Say, Jack—By the way . . . Did I Beat the draft?

SABBATH: *(To* DAVON.*)* You Married again.

DAVON: Wha'?

JACKSON: Rachael-uhs First.

SABBATH: Like, You two got married at some Nudist Church!

YEWELL: Hello! I Got it!

DAVON: Huh?

YEWELL: This MicroScheme—See! He brought y'all back . . . *(Points at* SABBATH.*)* After She got conceived!

RACHAEL: *(Hard-nosed.)* So?

YEWELL: SO? That makes Sabbath the Key!

DAVON: *(To* SABBATH.*)* What's her name?

SABBATH: Who?

DAVON: My-Your stepmother?

SABBATH: Jean.

JACKSON: *(To* YEWELL.*)* Boy, 'yer sure a Handful.

YEWELL: *(Smiles.)* I'm just "expediting" friend.

RACHAEL: *(To* JACKSON.*)* Did "Jean" Help him Mourn my passing?

JACKSON: *(Shakes head.)* Widow'd five years 'fore they wed.

SABBATH: *(To* RACHAEL.*)* She's cool! You'd hella like her, Mom. Her maiden name is Nash!

JACKSON: *(Of* DAVON.*)* Spent dem five years at t'is Commune where—

SABBATH: Dad, You invented Stash!

DAVON: *(To* JACKSON.*)* I did? (JACKSON *nods.)*

YEWELL: No shit?

JACKSON: *(To* DAVON.*)* Yep.

YEWELL: Cool!

DAVON: What's Stash?

SABBATH: These Fake Household items designed to hide Cash.

YEWELL: Like Soda cans and Ice cube Trays.

SABBATH: My Favorite one's the Soap!

DAVON: Soap?

SABBATH: Yep! On a Rope—

YEWELL: But, the Bar's Hollowed out.

SABBATH: See, It hangs by the tub—

YEWELL: So the Back side Conceals—

SABBATH: This like Cork you remove—

YEWELL: To store Valuables in.

DAVON: Man! Who woulda "thought"?

YEWELL: Quite a Coup, Mister D.

DAVON: I used to stash Grass in a box 'a Saltines . . .

RACHAEL: Say! How 'bout a "chick" Who no longer Breathes air?

DAVON: Aw, Gee Raych, I wish—That You coulda been there.

YEWELL: *(To* DAVON *of self.)* Then Just let the "Master" . . . *(To* TM*)* Re-program This Crate.

DAVON: Um, Jack—Any Chance?

JACKSON: Can't b' Toyin' wi' Fate.

RACHAEL: Oh? What's there to Lose?

SABBATH: Like, at Least take a shot!

YEWELL: The Girl's Life is at stake!

DAVON: *(Corrects* YEWELL.*)* Mrs. D.

SABBATH: *(To* JACKSON.*)* Have a Heart!

JACKSON: ul-Since Y'all're here on 'is "double" first Date . . . uh-Reckon m' Heart 'as put in 'eh Right place.

YEWELL: True—for a "novice" . . . You've done Very well. But Dude, circuits Buckle When I'm at the Helm.

JACKSON: Boy—'s Out 'a 'da question . . .

RACHAEL: And Who're You—God?

DAVON: s'Unrighteous, man!

SABBATH: Hella!

YEWELL: I-uh, Count . . . *(Collates.)* 4 to 1?

JACKSON: We All gotta swallow 'at bad wif' 'eh good, cause 'a Time don't abide by Majority rules . . . Fer Each cycle Nature see'd fit t' begin, plumb Hell 'r High Water must Come t' 'eh End.

RACHAEL: But What If the doctors were hip to my doom?

SABBATH: Yeah, They could perform—like a C-Section, dude!

JACKSON: Look! She's born, You die, 'n He invents Stash.

DAVON: I'm "real" sorry Raych.

RACHAEL: Stuff Stash up your Ass!

JACKSON: Now'll Gain more b' easin' than latherin' up . . . Sit Down, Have some Beans.

RACHAEL: Is this Bogus 'r What!

YEWELL: *(To* RACHAEL.*)* Bully!

DAVON: *(To* YEWELL.*)* Man, Cool it! Like—You're "one" to Talk.

JACKSON: *(To* DAVON.*)* uh-Like 'im 'r not, At's 'yer Soon Son-in-law.

Pause. All look at YEWELL.

SABBATH: *(To* JACKSON.*)* I Marry "Him"? *(*JACKSON *nods.)*

RACHAEL: Ha!

DAVON: *(Warns* YEWELL.*)* My Daughter wears Clothes!

YEWELL: I'll Cherish her, Sir.

SABBATH: Like—in "two" words: "I Don't!"

RACHAEL: *(To* JACKSON.*)* So, What happens Now?

JACKSON: Gonna Fill up 'at drum.

SABBATH: *(To* DAVON.*)* Huh?

DAVON: Sab, We're low on water.

SABBATH: Oh.

RACHAEL: *(To* JACKSON.*)* I meant—with Us.

JACKSON: Heh, You folks "relax" Now—Don't need Any help.

YEWELL: *(To* RACHAEL.*)* Accommodating—

RACHAEL: *(To* YEWELL.*)* —Ain't He.

YEWELL: Must "need" Something else.

DAVON: *(To* SABBATH.*)* So I own—What? Two cars?

SABBATH: Three!

DAVON: Wow.

RACHAEL: What's the Hitch, Jack?

JACKSON: Can't No one go Farther 'an where they was at.

YEWELL: *(To* RACHAEL.*)* Phase-Lift.

RACHAEL: *(To* YEWELL.*)* A Problem?

YEWELL: Nah, Mere child's play.

SABBATH: *(To* DAVON.*)* Like—Dad, You're a Socialite!

DAVON: Man, No Fucking Way!

Blackout.

Audio: Creaking sound of wheels rise from JACKSON'S *water cart.*

JACKSON, RACHAEL *and* SABBATH *exit on trail* YEWELL *(*SR*) and* DAVON
   *(*SL*) sit down* US *to fire.*

End Stage 3.

STAGE 4:
(partners)

Audio continues, with sound of creaking wheels. On audio, RACHAEL and
SABBATH (on walk) chime in.

VOICEOVER SABBATH: Look, There's Jackson . . . Howdy, Jackson!

Squeaking stops.

VOICEOVER JACKSON: Where Y'all headin'?

VOICEOVER SABBATH: I want to see the Buffaloes!

VOICEOVER RACHAEL: She wants to see the Buffaloes.

VOICEOVER SABBATH: We'll be back!

VOICEOVER JACKSON: You Gals have Fun!

VOICEOVER RACHAEL: Ciao.

Audio sound of squeaking wheels start up again.

VOICEOVER JACKSON: One more trip . . . 'n—uh'll be done.

Audio of squeaking wheels fades.

Lights on stage: afternoon (SL) sun light up sharp.

DAVON: Come on Man, You're jivin' me! Grass costs How Much?

YEWELL: 4,000 a pound—

DAVON: Wow! Must be "killer" stuff!

YEWELL: Mega-way Potent, sir . . . Nothing but "bud."

DAVON: You mean, like—No stems?

YEWELL: Sí. Two bowls: You're dust.

DAVON: So, What else like "happens"?

YEWELL: Oh, Nixon resigns.

DAVON: My wife's for McGovern!

YEWELL: He Won by Landslide.

DAVON: And the War?

YEWELL: Vietnam?

DAVON: Yeah?

YEWELL: We conquered 'em.

DAVON: Great!

YEWELL: *(Gaining steam.)* And Then It becomes . . . Our 51st State!

DAVON: Unreal! The whole Country?

YEWELL: The Beaches are "rad"!

DAVON: Man, What about Music?

YEWELL: Mm . . . *(Leans back.)* Funny you'd Ask.

DAVON: Funny? Why funny?

YEWELL: Cause Music's my Life!

DAVON: But Hey! I thought you were like, some kine 'a Spy?

Audio: Squeaking noise rises slow from behind, while unseen JACKSON *approaches with second barrel of water.*

YEWELL: Means to an End.

DAVON: Listen, Here comes ole' Jack. Takes 'm three trips to fill.

YEWELL: He's got one more and back.

Squeaking noise continues rising.

DAVON: Like-uh You in a Band?

YEWELL: Nahh—Can't stand the Hype.

DAVON: So Whaddaya "play"?

YEWELL: Well, "mostly" I Write.

Squeaking noise stops.

DAVON: Songs?

YEWELL: *(Nods.)* Yes Indeed, Sir. Eleven went "gold."

DAVON: Yeah?

YEWELL: And One earned a Grammy.

DAVON: No!

YEWELL: *(Grandsitting.)* "We Are The World."

Pause.

Audio: Sound of JACKSON *filling water drum from barrel.*

DAVON: This planet, man . . . S' Full 'a Soul. We "are" the World!
S' Righteous Bro!

YEWELL: *(Sings.)* We Are The World . . .

DAVON: Say, Groove on Out!

YEWELL: *(Sings.)* We Are The Children . . .

DAVON: *(Harmonizing counterpart.)* Equal Children . . .

YEWELL: We Are (The)— . . . *(Stops.)*

DAVON: *(Chimes in on "The")* — (The) Freedom Every Human Being That's Born Deserves! We Are . . . What's next?—

YEWELL: The "world."

DAVON: Right on! We Are . . .

Sound of water stops.

YEWELL: Curious.

DAVON: uh—'Bout What?

YEWELL: *(Jerks head at TM. Sings.)* That "machine."

DAVON: *(Looks at TM.)* Yeah. Man, I dig your tune . . .

YEWELL: Keen ear.

DAVON: We "are" the World!

Pause.

Audio sound of squeaking wheels begins then fades off in the distance.

YEWELL: *(Crossing SL.)* uh-Cat's "away."

DAVON: Huh?

YEWELL: Jack is gone.

DAVON: Oh.

YEWELL: Mice'll Play.

DAVON: Another Song?

YEWELL: *(Clutching throat.)* Sir, a-hem . . . My Chords're Fried.

DAVON: *(Looking in boat hole.)* This Boat's a Mess!

YEWELL: *(Leaning against boat.)* Let's go Inside.

DAVON: *(Backs off.)* Uh . . .

Pause.

YEWELL: *(Enters boat.)* Come on!

DAVON: *(Hesitates.)* Man, I don't know.

YEWELL: Tell Jack we had to find some bowls. *(Disappears into boat.)*

DAVON: *(Enters boat; looks down* SR.*)* Hey! *(Picks up bowls.)* Here they are!

YEWELL: Okay, a Fork!

DAVON: *(Setting down bowls.)* Wait!

YEWELL: Look at This!

DAVON: *(Disappearing.)* It's kine 'a dark.

RACHAEL *and* SABBATH *approach from trail.*

SABBATH: *(Offstage.)* I can't believe—They're hella Free. *(Appears* US *at end of trail.)* It's Awesome, Mom!

RACHAEL: *(Passing* SABBATH.*)* What's up his sleeve?

Pause. RACHAEL *and* SABBATH *stop* CS.

RACHAEL: *(Looking around.)* Ha!

SABBATH: Like, What happened?

RACHAEL: Should 'a "known."

SABBATH: Where's Dad?

RACHAEL: Your father's prob'ly hiding just in case Jack needs a hand.

SABBATH: So—What should we do?

RACHAEL: Sabbath—Go with the Flow! *(Dances.)*

SABBATH: Hey Mom, Can you like Teach me how to do the um 'a Go-Go?

RACHAEL: The Go-Go?

SABBATH: Please?

RACHAEL: Mm. Been a while. *(Moves left foot—*SABBATH *does same.) Moves right foot—*SABBATH *does same. Bends both knees—*SABBATH *does same.)* Left foot . . . Right foot . . . Drop . . . *(Holds pose.)*

SABBATH: *(Holding same pose.)* My roommate Thalia's gonna Flip, Mom. This is Really Hot!

RACHAEL: Hey—Pick a song!

SABBATH: Huh?

RACHAEL: In your mind.

SABBATH: Oh! umm . . . B-b-b-b-Bad To The Bone!

RACHAEL: hm-Had to be After my time.

SABBATH: uh-I'm Not Your Stepping Stone?

RACHAEL: Yeah, That'll do!

SABBATH: You like the Monkees?

RACHAEL: Used to, As a "kid." Blew my mind when I found out They weren't even "real"!

SABBATH: *(Moves left foot.)* Left foot?

RACHAEL: *(Moves right foot.)* Right foot . . .

SABBATH: Drop!

RACHAEL: *(Shaking fists above head.)* Shake Your Fists! Up!

SABBATH *follows.*

RACHAEL AND SABBATH: *(Sing and dance: left foot, then right foot.)* I–I–I–I–I'm . . . Not—Your . . . *(Both drop.)* Stepping Stone . . . *(Both shake fists and rise.)*

RACHAEL: Okay—Turn ! *(Both turn 180 degrees and continue dancing.)*

SABBATH: *(In sync with bridge of song.)* It's—you know, Hella weird . . . When like you Lose your Mom . . . Especially for girls . . . Who way depend more on Role Models . . . But Dad and Jean were always "there" . . . And Tang, My therapist . . . I've got a younger half-brother. *(Pause.)* His name is Chris!

RACHAEL: Turn! *(Both turn 180 degrees and continue dancing.)*

RACHAEL AND SABBATH: *(Facing each other; sing-dance in unison.)* I–I–I–I–I'm Not Your Stepping Stone . . . *(Both repeat.)*

Audio: Squeaking noise now faintly bodes JACKSON's *final load.*

RACHAEL: Turn! *(Both turn 180 degrees and continue dancing.)*

SABBATH: *(In sync with bridge of song.)* I bought, Like, this book . . . How to Manage Grief . . .

Quick flash of colored lights shoot out from TM.

Pause.

Audio: Squeaking noise of JACKSON *rises.*

RACHAEL *and* SABBATH *turn us.*

DAVON: *(Inside boat. Scared.)* Hurry! *(Exits boat.)* Quick! *(Crossing* DSR.*)*

RACHAEL: wh-Fuck was That?

YEWELL: *(Appears in hole.)* Eureka!

DAVON: *(Stopping* SR *behind fire.)* Man . . . *(Turns to* YEWELL.*)* He's Comin' Back!

RACHAEL: *(To* YEWELL.*)* Any luck?

YEWELL: *(Beams.)* We "own" this Crate!

SABBATH: But Jackson said—

YEWELL: That Dude's a Flake!

Audio: Squeaking noise ends.

DAVON: Hey, Yewell's Right Man. If Jack's From the Past, Then How'd "he" go farther than where We were At?

Audio: Sound of JACKSON *dumping buckets of water into drum begins.*

RACHAEL: Yeah!

SABBATH: Like—

YEWELL: Touché, Sir!

SABBATH: He "knew"!

RACHAEL: We've been Had!

SABBATH: *(Of* YEWELL.*)* I Marry "him"!

DAVON: He Lied to us, Sab.

Audio: Sound of JACKSON *dumping water continues.*

YEWELL: *(Exits boat.)* Group! Form a Blockade . . . *(Turns* US *raising hands.)* Here. uh-Sabbath. You First . . . *(*SABBATH *crosses* DSL. *Smiles turning* SL *to* RACHAEL. *Places left hand on* RACHAEL'S *shoulder.)* Then You, Mrs. D.

Sound of JACKSON *dumping water stops.*

RACHAEL: Take your Hand off me Twirp!

YEWELL: *(Removing hand.)* Heh . . . *(Turns to* DAVON.*)* Sir . . . *(Points.)* There . . . *(*DAVON *takes position.)* Then Me . . . *(Crosses* US.*)*

JACKSON *appears at end of trail.*

SABBATH: Like, Chill out! *(Whispers.)* Here he comes!

DAVON: So Where do we Stand?

RACHAEL: *(Crossing into position.)* Tell the Truth Jack, Or Else!

JACKSON: *(Approaching* DS. *To self.)* Ol-drum's fit t' Bust . . . *(Looks at group.)* Heh . . . *(Stops* SL.*)* How 'r y' Folks, Gettin' on? *(Pause. Shuffles.)* Y'all want some Beans? *(Smiles from* SABBATH *to* YEWELL.*)*

SABBATH: Where Are You "from"?

JACKSON *looks from* YEWELL *to* SABBATH.

Blackout.

Audio: Sound of chickens squawking begins.

DAVON *sits* SL *of fire facing* SR; SABBATH *sits* USR *to* DAVON *facing* DSC. JACKSON *sits a tad more* SL *than before—facing out behind fire.* YEWELL *sits in hole—blocking entrance to boat.* RACHAEL *sits* DSL—*cordoning* JACKSON *off.*

End Stage 4.

STAGE 5:
(premise)

Audio: Squawking fades.

Scene: Campfire, noon and boat entry lights up.

SABBATH: Come on!

YEWELL: Give It Up!

RACHAEL: No more Lies!

DAVON: Yeah!

SABBATH: What year?

JACKSON: *(Hems.)* Uhh . . . *(Drops accent.)* 20-22.

DAVON: Wow!

RACHAEL: Ha!

YEWELL: Some Pioneer.

SABBATH: So, What—Like . . . *(Points at* TM.) You "lease" That?

JACKSON: *(Shakes head.)* Invented My "own."

RACHAEL: *(Disbelieving.)* Right!

YEWELL: *(To* RACHAEL.) Accent 'n All.

JACKSON: *(Turns to* SABBATH.) To Help Someone I love . . .

DAVON: *(To* SABBATH.) Love's Righteous.

RACHAEL: *(To* YEWELL *of* DAVON.) He bought It.

YEWELL: *(To* DAVON.) Sir, How 'bout a Bridge?

SABBATH: *(To* JACKSON.*)* Who is She?

DAVON: You shacked Up?

JACKSON: *(To* SABBATH.*)* Your daughter, Justine.

SABBATH: *(To* JACKSON.*)* Me?

YEWELL: *(To* JACKSON.*)* Mine?

JACKSON: Yep!

SABBATH: *(To* JACKSON *of* YEWELL.*)* His?

DAVON: Who?

RACHAEL: *(To* DAVON *of* SABBATH *and* YEWELL.*)* Their daughter.

JACKSON: *(Slowly—to self.)* Justine . . .

DAVON: *(To* JACKSON.*)* You mean, I'm a "granddad"?

JACKSON: *(Snaps out.)* Not Yet, son—We'll see.

SABBATH: *(To* JACKSON *of* YEWELL.*)* Did "he" like Drug me?

JACKSON: Nope, "mutual" Consent . . . *(To* RACHAEL *and* DAVON.*)* Went back t' her room, 'n then they had Sex.

DAVON: *(To* JACKSON *of* YEWELL.*)* What's wrong with "his" Place?

YEWELL: *(Jumps in.)* I'm airing it Out. The Walls were "just" Painted!

JACKSON: Boy sleeps on a Couch.

RACHAEL: Ha!

YEWELL: Doctor's Orders. My Spine's hella Fucked. Tried "every" Mattress—All of them Suck!

JACKSON:

When I first met your daughter, in the fall of '16 . . .
I'd just turned 31 . . . She was all of 18.
Though Work kept me Caged-up inside M.I.T.
One day in the Square . . . She sat down Next to me.

(Pause.)

She said the word, "Autumn" . . . I asked, "That your name?"
She said, "No, It's a Season—When Leaves turn to Flame."
"Sounds like a Song," I said. She asked "By Who?"
"Whom" I corrected her . . . She laughed, "Dumb rule."

DAVON: Wow! He's got each Word "committed" to Mind.

JACKSON: I've Relived that moment, Son—So many Times.

RACHAEL: First thing Davon said was, "Can I have Your Soul?"

SABBATH: uh-Yewell asked me if the Lunchroom was full.

JACKSON: Justine was a Freshman at nearby U Mass. Her Major was Sonics for SatelliteTrax.

DAVON: NASA?

SABBATH: The "hedgehog"?

YEWELL: Seattle?

RACHAEL: Booms?

JACKSON: V.A.M.P.

RACHAEL, DAVON, SABBATH & YEWELL: Huh?

JACKSON: Visual/Audio-Modal/Pro-Tem. *(Pause.)* V.A.M.P.'s the new Home Multi-Media Base . . . Select any SideTrack, It's Beamed in from Space.

DAVON: *(To JACKSON.)* Say What? You mean 8-track?

YEWELL: uh-Sir . . . *(Makes sign of cross.)* Rest in Peace.

DAVON: *(Bummed.)* Life's Over!

YEWELL: *(Impassively consoles* DAVON.*)* That's Progress.

JACKSON: *(Inspired.)* You Program your "needs."

SABBATH: *(To* JACKSON.*)* Like, Movies?

JACKSON: Darn Tootin. There's even Quik Shop! You move down the aisles 'n Click what you want.

YEWELL: *(To* JACKSON.*)* How much?

JACKSON: Seven thousand.

DAVON: Man, Not in my Dreams!

RACHAEL: It's Pseudo "control"!

SABBATH: *(To* JACKSON.*)* Like, What's Up with Justine?

JACKSON: We met Everyday . . . Fell in Love.

YEWELL: *(To* RACHAEL.*)* Song and dance.

JACKSON: I had my Research.

RACHAEL: *(To* YEWELL.*)* Bet She "wore" the Pants.

DAVON: Like, What kine 'a "research"?

JACKSON: The Conversion of Time. We moved in Together, man . . . Life was Sublime. She didn't want Marraige . . . No paper, just "us." The Ideal arrangement . . . Our Love was enough . . . *(To* SABBATH.*)* I met you One Christmas . . .

SABBATH: Yeah?

YEWELL: *(To* JACKSON.*)* What about Me?

JACKSON: *(To* YEWELL.*)* Um—Sabbath divorced you Way back 'n aught three. *(Pause.)* Spent two Blissful years . . . Hogs rollin' 'n Mud . . . then Doctors found something Wrong . . . with Justine's blood . . . *(Pause.)* Plasmacytoma—Cancerous cells . . . Inside her Bloodstream . . . Hard to Expel.

(Long pause.)

Though she seemed Full of Hope . . . I could See the "disease" in her Taking its Toll . . . So I promised to Save her. "Don't worry. You'll See!" 'N worked like a Dog, to perfect My machine. See— if We could go Back where She still had her Health, Then Maybe the Doctors . . . *(Softly.)* could . . . *(Chokes.)* 's-How it was Dealt . . .

Pause.

JACKSON *laments.*

YEWELL: Guess 'ole Jack blew it . . .

JACKSON: I'll Never give Up! 'At's Why y'all 'r Here!

SABBATH: *(Confused.)* Like-uh, How can We help?

JACKSON: *(To* SABBATH.*)* By–um—"reenacting" the Blessed Event.

SABBATH: You Mean—Have the Baby?

JACKSON: *(Smiles at* SABBATH.*)* Well?

YEWELL: Partner—I'm There!

Blackout.

Audio: Comic fiddle version of "Turkey In The Straw" begins.

DAVON, SABBATH *and* YEWELL *enter boat.*

RACHAEL *kneels* SL *of* JACKSON.

End Stage 5.

STAGE 6:
(prospect)

Audio: "Turkey" fades.

Setting: Campfire, afternoon and boat entry lights up sharp.

JACKSON: ul-First off I went back, to 2018 . . . Cocksure 'at m' Forelock'd bail out Justine.

RACHAEL   You just Showed up?

JACKSON: Outside 'r Door.

DAVON *appears backing up inside boat.*

RACHAEL: Like What'd she Do?

JACKSON: *(Smiles.)* 'Bout hit 'de Floor!

DAVON: *(Turning around—stops in hole.)* uh-Say I "think" They're Almost done.

JACKSON: *(Looks at DAVON.)* 'At's fine, uh . . . Keep me posted, Son.

DAVON *looks back in boat—then nods to* JACKSON, *and disappears again.*

RACHAEL: Look, You tell the Doctors—My "status" Up Front . . . And I'll bet They won't let My uterus Bust!

JACKSON: Take it from Me see, We tried Everything . . . From daily Transfusions t' Primal Healin' . . . All came t' Naught though— Them cells re-occurred.

RACHAEL: But That doesn't put Me in the same boat as Her.

JACKSON: Wound up Goin' back then, t' When we first Met—Over 'n over 'n over Agin.

RACHAEL: Must 'a got Old, Jack.

JACKSON: Not 'n the Least. Moments with Her . . . Elapsed as we Pleased.

RACHAEL: Guess that explains Why You're "here" by Yourself.

JACKSON: Don't you think Rachael's maligned Jack Enough?

RACHAEL: *(Drooping shoulders.)* Alright . . . *(Flutters eyelashes.)* I'll be "passive." Provided—

JACKSON: I What?

RACHAEL: *(Leans to* JACKSON.*)* One: Warn My Doctor.

JACKSON: Dad-burn!

RACHAEL: *(Leans back.)* Two: Can the "drawl."

JACKSON: Did I "not" Say Her Sickness Resumed?

RACHAEL: She had a Disease, Not a Clot in her Womb.

JACKSON: Bound and determined to save Her somehow, My days were spent Scouting the "past" for Locales . . . Strange as it Seems, These "plains" proffered Hope . . . So I brought Justine "here" 'n We lived in this Boat.

RACHAEL: I "gather" she Died.

Pause.

JACKSON: Same painful Way . . . She's buried nearby . . . Got a Stone on her Grave . . . *(Reverting to drawl.)* But See, Here's m' Pickle—

RACHAEL: *(Mocking.)* Shit Howdy—Hot Damn!

JACKSON: Hey—When in Rome?

RACHAEL: *(In* JACKSON's *drawl.)* Run like Hell if 'yer a "Christian"!

JACKSON: Because she Died one hundred fifty years before She did, Now it Means that up ahead, Justine never "existed."

RACHAEL: So you . . . Ahhh, Yeah—Now I get it!

JACKSON: Only chance I Got.

RACHAEL: If I don't give "birth" to Sabbath, You'll be Truly fucked!

JACKSON: Justine said She wished Her Mom's Mom hadn't Died . . . So I thought it "just" to extend You this Time.

RACHAEL: My Oh My, Aren't We generous? I want to Live, man! How 'bout My Wish?

Pause.

DAVON *appears and exits boat.*

JACKSON: How'd it Go?

DAVON: *(Stopping* CSL *between* RACHAEL *and* JACKSON.*)* Guess Everything's cool.

RACHAEL: What could be Cool about Sleeping with "Yewell"?

Pause.

YEWELL *appears and stops in boat hole.*

YEWELL: The Eagle has "landed."

JACKSON: Where's Sabbath?

YEWELL: *(Hitching up pants.)* The Lady's still catching her Breath.

RACHAEL: Ha!

DAVON: *(To* RACHAEL.*)* What, Raych?

RACHAEL: Prob'ly sick to her Stomach.

DAVON: No, she's Alright. She just Needed some Space.

YEWELL: *(Crossing* SR *from boat behind* RACHAEL *and* JACKSON.*)* Speaking of Space— *(Squats between* RACHAEL *and* JACKSON.*)* Jack, Here's an Idea . . .

SABBATH: *(Appears—stops in hole.)* Like, I've "transcended"!

YEWELL: Why wait 20 Years?

JACKSON: What now? You Lost me.

YEWELL: Just Beam on Ahead, And If she's not Healthy, We'll try it Again!

JACKSON: Mmm . . .

RACHAEL: But?

YEWELL: *(Nudging* RACHAEL.*)* Don't Blow it! *(To* JACKSON.*)* Well?

JACKSON: Seems worth a shot.

SABBATH: *(Needing attention.)* Like I've "transcended."

YEWELL: *(To* JACKSON.*)* So?

JACKSON: Why the hell not?

YEWELL: *(Rising.)* Jackson is Leaving!

DAVON: Now?

JACKSON: *(Rising.)* Won't be for long.

SABBATH: *(To* DAVON.*)* Do I look "transcended"?

DAVON: Uh . . .

YEWELL: *(Patting* JACKSON's *shoulder.)* Good luck!

DAVON: *(To* SABBATH. *Looks at* RACHAEL.*)* Ask your Mom.

JACKSON *crosses to entry.*

JACKSON: 'Scuse me there, Sabbath.

YEWELL: Please! Destiny waits!

SABBATH *exits boat.* JACKSON *enters boat.*

DAVON: *(To* YEWELL.*)* Man, Where's he Going?

YEWELL: Sir, Out of the way.

SABBATH: *(To* RACHAEL.*)* Do I look "transcended"?

RACHAEL: How big was his schlong?

SABBATH: *(Blushing.)* Mom, I'm embarrassed.

RACHAEL: Well?

SABBATH: *(Smiles.)* More like, How "small"!

JACKSON: *(Exits boat crossing* SL *to* TM.*)* You folks, Have some Beans.

YEWELL: uh-All Systems Go?

SABBATH: S'up Dad?

DAVON: He's Splitting.

JACKSON: *(Standing with back parallel to* TM.*)* Be Back 'fore you Know.

Audio: Weird hum starts rising slow.

RACHAEL: *(Not looking.)* Ciao!

YEWELL: Keep in Touch Dude!

JACKSON: *(Looks up.)* Justine, Here I Come!

SABBATH: *(To* DAVON.*)* Like, Think we should Wave?

DAVON: *(Waves.)* um-I guess so . . .

SABBATH: *(Waves.)* Have Fun!

Blackout.

Colored light beams shoot out from TM.

JACKSON *exits.*

Audio: Weird hum fades.

Campfire, afternoon and boat entry lights up.

SABBATH: S'Anyone Hungry?

YEWELL: Got No time to Eat. *(Enters boat.)*

DAVON: *(Into boat.)* Man, What's your "big" Hurry?

SABBATH: Mom?

RACHAEL: Don't look at Me.

DAVON: *(To self.)* Something's sure Fishy! *(To* SABBATH.*)* So-uh . . . *(Looks at* RACHAEL—*lowers voice.)* Jean's pretty cool?

YEWELL *exits boat.*

SABBATH: Way Dad, She's Hella!

DAVON: Um's, that like Beaucoup?

RACHAEL: What gives?

YEWELL: *(Squats* SL *to* RACHAEL.*)* No Problem!

RACHAEL: I'm dead in 9 months!

SABBATH: Beaucoup's same as Hella.

YEWELL: *(Checks* DAVON *and* SABBATH. *Whispers to* RACHAEL.*)* We're Blowin' this dump!

DAVON: Sab, What's "transcended"?

SABBATH: Uhhm . . .

RACHAEL: *(To* YEWELL *of* DAVON *and* SABBATH.*)* What about "them"?

SABBATH: It means Like . . .

YEWELL: Don't worry, I-uh "faked" Orgasm.

SABBATH: Go Beyond the Limits of.

RACHAEL: Oh Really?

DAVON: Wow!

YEWELL: *(Looks at* DAVON *and* SABBATH.*)* It worked!

DAVON: Sab?

RACHAEL: *(Beckons to* YEWELL *crossing* US *to boat entry.)* Come On!

DAVON: That's "hella" Righteous.

RACHAEL: *(Stops* SR *of entry. Seducing* YEWELL.*)* My Turn!

YEWELL *saunters* US *to boat hole.*

SABBATH: Thanks, Dad.

YEWELL: *(Stops near boat hole.)* Ladies First.

RACHAEL *leads* YEWELL *in boat by belt in boat.*

DAVON: How have you "transcended"?

SABBATH: I'm like "nurturing" Justine. So now I Have a "purpose." Be the Best Mom I can Be . . .

DAVON: I'm "proud" of you, Sab.

RACHAEL: *(Appears in boat hole.)* And don't forget the Guns.

YEWELL: *(Sticking head out of boat hole.)* Okay Okay, I got it.

RACHAEL: *(Stops at* TM. *Waves to* DAVON *and* SABBATH.*)* See you Later! Gotta Run!

Audio: Weird hum rises.

DAVON: Wait!

SABBATH: Mom!

DAVON: Where you Going?

RACHAEL: To buy Hot Dogs for them Beans.

Pause.

DAVON *and* SABBATH *turn to each other, shrug—turn back to* RACHAEL *and wave.*

RACHAEL: *(Tasting power.)* Only this time They "will" Win!

Blackout.

Colored light beams shoot out from machine.

RACHAEL *exits.*

Audio: Weird hum fades.

Campfire, afternoon and boat entry lights up.

SABBATH: Dad, You like Hot Dogs?

DAVON: You bet, Sab! They're "cheap."

SABBATH: Well, Jean never Buys them. She doesn't "eat" Meat.

DAVON: *(Crossing* US *to boat.)* What's Yewell up to, man? *(Peeks in.)* Prob'ly no good.

Red light rises above SABBATH.

SABBATH: *(Looks up.)* Hey Thalia, I'm "pregnant"!

DAVON *enters boat—stops.*

Blackout—save red light.

Audio: New squeak sound begins.

SABBATH: Of course, I'm like "sure"!

Red light out. SABBATH *exits. Squeak ends.*

Campfire, afternoon and boat entry lights up.

DAVON: *(Turns to* SABBATH.*)* Sit tight, Sab. *(Turns back—stops.)* She's gone, man! *(Turns around.)* Hey! *(Exits boat.)* Sab? Where'd you Go?

YEWELL *exits boat.*

DAVON: What happened to my Daughter, Man?

YEWELL: *(Stops at* TM*—turning back parallel to it.)* Dude—Wouldn't Even know.

Audio: Weird hum rises.

DAVON: If I find out you're Lying!

YEWELL: Look, You "won't." You have My word . . . Guess I'll catch you later—"Davon."

DAVON: What Happppened, like—to Sir?

Blackout.

Colored light beams shoot out from TM.
YEWELL *exits.*

Audio: Weird hum ends.

Audio of JACKSON *talking to self 20 years ahead begins (accompanied by crickets.)*

DAVON *sits* DS *to fire,* JACKSON *enters and stands parallel to* TM.

End Stage 6.

STAGE 7:
(progress)

Audio: JACKSON's *voice continues. Sound of shuffling through the weeds.*

JACKSON: Hm, No grave. Means one of two Things: Justine's gone Elsewhere, Or I've been "hoodwinked"! *(Walks back to camp through weeds.)* Who's kidding Who "whom,"—Ahhh, Justine. I'm letting your Dad do, what Wasn't in "me." Look on the Bright side—Life's better Alone . . . *(Enters path. Sound of weeds stop.)* At least Life without "you" . . . *(Pause. Arrives at camp.)* Time to go.

Audio: Weird hum begins.

Colored light beams shoot out from TM.

Audio: Weird hum fades.

Campfire, moon and boat entry lights up.

DAVON: Hey, Jack! You seen Sabbath?

JACKSON: Justine weren't "there." I waited.

DAVON: She vanished—like, into thin Air.

JACKSON: *(Looks around.)* hm-Where are the Others?

DAVON: They did the Time thing. Raych went for Hot Dogs to go with your Beans!

JACKSON: And Yewell?

DAVON: He split with Some "weird" kine 'a Map

JACKSON: Boy stole my MicroScheme!

DAVON: Bummertime, Jack.

JACKSON: You say Sabbath "vanished"?

DAVON: Yeah! Here, man—Then "gone."

JACKSON: Promise fulfilled.

DAVON: What the hell Que Paso'ed?

JACKSON: See, Rachael fixed "things" so yer' Daughter Ain't born.

DAVON: That transcends Uncool!

JACKSON: ul-You Can't blame 'r Son. She wanted t' "live," no Matter 'a cost.

DAVON: But Sabbath's "unique"!

JACKSON: Same as Everyone, Hos.

Pause.

JACKSON: Say-um, Lookie here—Let's make a Deal.

DAVON: You seen that Show Man? It's Hella Unreal!

JACKSON: *(Entering boat.)* Come on. We got Work.

DAVON: *(Alarmed.)* Work? Man—My Checks!

JACKSON: Easy, Son.

DAVON: But if—

JACKSON: No one'll know.

DAVON: What?

JACKSON: Remake Sabbath.

DAVON: Done!

Pause. JACKSON *exits into boat.* DAVON *follows* JACKSON.

JACKSON: *(Inside boat.)* Then You can Go . . . Wherever you Want.

DAVON: *(Inside boat.)* Anywhere?

JACKSON: Name it.

DAVON: Can I "sit" up Front?

Pause.

Audio: Weird hum begins.

JACKSON: *(Exits boat)* All set?

DAVON: *(Exits boat, crossing to* TM.*)* Man, I'm Going!

JACKSON: Uhh . . . *(Turns to* DAVON.*)* Like to come "back"?

DAVON: *(Turning parallel to* TM.*)* Anytime.

JACKSON: Bye, Son.

DAVON: *(Salutes.)* Later on . . . Jack.

Blackout.

Colored light beams shoot out from TM.

DAVON *exits.*

Audio: Weird hum ends.

Campfire, moon and boat entry lights up.

JACKSON: hm, Guess I could 'a left well enough Alone . . . but I knew 'n m' Heart what all has t' be "done" . . . Yewell's the one 'At shouldn't get "born."

Pause. Enters boat, disappears. Opens TM *screen; video begins.*

JACKSON: Yep, she ain't Pregnant. Hm . . . Little Bighorn.

THIRD PHASE:
(Video)

Little Bighorn, Dakota; 1876.

SHOT 1: MEDIUM
RACHAEL *(dressed in squaw outfit) sifts through duffel bag full of pistols.*

SITTING BULL *sits on stump facing* RACHAEL *with a leer.*

LITTLE THORN *stands* SR *to* SITTING BULL *with arms folded stoically.*

RACHAEL: *(Pulling out an automatic.)* Here Chief, Look at This . . . *(Holds up gun to* SITTING BULL.*)* Holds 8 rounds in the Clip.

SHOT 2: CLOSE UP OF RACHAEL, SITTING BULL AND GUN

RACHAEL: *(Demonstrates.)* All you do is "squeeze" the Trigger. *(Gives gun to* SITTING BULL.*)* Now . . . Be Careful.

SITTING BULL *promptly points gun at* LITTLE THORN.

SHOT 3: LITTLE THORN (FROM TORSO UP)

Gunshot. Bullet enters LITTLE THORN'S *chest;* LITTLE THORN *falls from frame.*

RACHAEL: *(Off camera.)* Shit!

SHOT 4: TIGHTER VERSION OF SHOT 1

RACHAEL: *(Grabbing gun from* SITTING BULL.*)* No Chief! Not "your" People, man. The Paleface. Enemy!

SITTING BULL: *(Staring down at* LITTLE THORN'S *corpse.)* Don't Worry. *(Turns to* RACHAEL, *flips right hand at* LITTLE THORN'S *corpse.)* Only "Brother-in-Law" . . . Been meaning to do that For Years!

SHOT 5: OVER CORPSE.

SITTING BULL: *(Off camera.)* Little Thorn, We meet Again at Happy Hunting Ground.

SHOT 6: ANGLED OVER RACHAEL'S LEFT SHOULDER

RACHAEL: *(Putting gun back in bag.)* So Chief . . . *(Looks at* SITTING BULL.*)* What should we do?

SITTING BULL: *(Sits up.)* Plan can Wait. *(Smacks lips.)* Let's get it On!

SHOT 7: CLOSE UP OF RACHAEL

RACHAEL: *(Agitated.)* Will you Forget that I'm a "woman" for just One Minute!

SHOT 8: CLOSE UP OF SITTING BULL

SITTING BULL: *(Smiling.)* Only Way to do "that" . . . is Marry You.

SHOT 9: SAME AS SHOT 1.

Audio: Weird hum begins.

RACHAEL: Ah Shit!

RACHAEL *dissolves with duffel bag.*

Audio: Weird hum ends.

SHOT 10: FULL-FRONT SITTING BULL

SITTING BULL: *(Concluding.)* hm . . . White Squaw not Sitting Bull's "type" . . . *(Aside.)* First thing Tomorrow —Give up Peace pipe!

End Third Phase Video.

Pause.

Onstage: JACKSON *appears in boat hole.*

JACKSON: Back to the sleeping bag, 3rd time with Davon . . .
    Best thing she does is give Life to Sabbath. Oh, yeah. *(Turns* SL.*)*
    Right uh- . . . *(Disappears.)* Vaporize guns. Perfect. Now Yewell.
    (Pause.) Los Angeles. Inventions Inc. 1995. *(Video begins.)* Plumb
    'bout t' Git hissef Took fer' a "ride."

FOURTH PHASE:
(Video)

Inventions Inc. Office. L.A.; 1995.

Two desks separated by cheap partition.

MAX *sits behind* SR *desk watching* BILLY MACHARAINA *dance the macharaina.*

YEWELL *sits facing* MOSHE'S *desk (*SL*) holding microscheme.*

SHOT 1: ANGLED OVER YEWELL'S LEFT SHOULDER FACING MOSHE

MOSHE: *(Sandbagging.)* You say it's a "time" machine?

YEWELL: *(Sets plan down on desk.)* My friend, The McCoy!

MOSHE: *(Eyeing plans.)* What's your name?

YEWELL: Yewell.

MOSHE: *(Rises out of frame. Stops beside* YEWELL. *Places left hand on*
    YEWELL'S *shoulder.)* Stay put!

YEWELL: Sure!

MOSHE *removes hand, leaves frame.*

SHOT 2: MOSHE FROM TORSO UP

MOSHE: *(Under breath.)* Dumb Goy.

SHOT 3: MAX'S OFFICE

MAX *sits watching* BILLY MACHARAINA *dance;* MOSHE *enters frame.*

MOSHE: Max!

MAX*:* *(Points to* BILLY.*)* Look!

MOSHE: *(Stops. Looks at* BILLY. *Unimpressed.)* He's dancing.

MAX: *(Kvetching.)* He's Billy Macharaina.

MOSHE: *(Turns to* MAX.*)* What's this?

MAX: *(Annoyed.)* Deaf? Macharaina!

BILLY: *(Dancing.)* From South America!

SHOT 5: FULL SL YEWELL IN PROFILE

YEWELL: *(Fantasizing headline.)* 20-year-old "Boy Wonder" . . . Richest
Man in "World" . . .

SHOT 6: ANGLED DSR ACROSS MAX'S DESK

BILLY—*from shoulders up*—dances SL out of frame.

MOSHE *enters frame* SL, *leans to* MAX *on side of desk.*

MOSHE: *(Urgent.)* Max, Look—Forget this Macha Macha.

SHOT 7: YEWELL'S FACE; FRONT—CLOSE UP

YEWELL: 50 Million "sold."

SHOT 8: TIGHTER VERSION OF SHOT 6

MAX: *(Clasping hands in front of chin.)* Moshe, No! *(Sits up.)* A Time Machine?

MOSHE *nods;* MAX *turns to* BILLY.

SHOT 9: FULL BILLY DANCING AGAINST WALL

MAX*:   (Off camera.)* Hey Macharaina! *(*BILLY *stops dancing. Turns to* MAX *with high hopes.)* We'll call you up next week. *(*BILLY'S *face falls. Turns and exits frame.)*

SHOT 10: YEWELL ANGLED FROM BEHIND MOSHE'S DESK

YEWELL: *(Picks up plans. Sings.)* I "rule" the World . . .

SHOT 11: SAME AS SHOT 8

MAX: *(Hands* MOSHE *microcamera.)* Here—Let me talk. *(*MOSHE *looks at microcamera.)*

SHOT 12: SAME AS SHOT 5

YEWELL: *(Sings.)* I "own" the People . . .

SHOT 13: MAX BEHIND MOSHE—LEAVING MAX'S OFFICE

MAX: You take Pictures. What's his name?

MOSHE: Schmuck.

SHOT 14: SAME AS SHOT 10

YEWELL *hums;* MAX *and* MOSHE *enter frame behind* YEWELL.

Audio: Weird hum begins.

YEWELL: *(Horrified.)* Oh No!

MOSHE: *(Cordial.)* Max . . .

MAX: What's this Buzzing?

MOSHE: How should I Know?

Pause.

Wincing, YEWELL *dissolves while clutching plans.*

Audio: Weird hum ends.

MAX: *(Listening.)* It's gone, Mosh.

MOSHE: *(Looks at empty chair.)* So's a Fortune, Max.

MAX: *(Looks at chair.)* Better get that Billy back! *(Runs out of frame.)*

MOSHE *follow* MAX.

SHOT 15: LOW—HALLWAY

MAX: *(Running past camera yelling.)* Macharaina!

MOSHE: *(Doing same.)* Macharaina!

SHOT 16: FULL—OPEN WINDOW; OUTSIDE BILLY (SMALL FIGURE) WALKS AWAY WITH HEAD HUNG

MAX: *(Entering frame* SL.) Couldn't be Far. *(Looks out window.)*

MOSHE *enters frame; stopping by window—looks out—sees* BILLY *across street.*

MAX*: (Shouts.)* Hey! Macharaina!

BILLY *stops, turns around and starts to dance.*

MAX: *(Looks at* MOSHE.*)* Who knows? It might catch on.

End Fourth Phase video.

JACKSON: *(Inside boat.)* If that Boy had His way . . . We'd be on Planet Yewell . . . So I'd say 'n This case . . . It's "kind" to be cruel. Conceived 1973. June the 19th. But Not "if" on That day His Mom's in "Peking" . . . *(Pause.)* ul-That's 'At, uhh—Any loose ends? *(Video begins.)* Oh Yeah Right, um . . . Keep the "Promise" That I made to Davon.

FIFTH PHASE:
(Video)

Same as Phase 1—Concert; Upstate New York.

SHOT 1: FULL—RACHAEL AND DAVON MAKING LOVE IN SLEEPING BAG

DAVON: *(Rolling off* RACHAEL.*)* Oh . . .

RACHAEL: *(Horrified.)* No!

Audio: Weird hum begins.

DAVON: How many Times We make "it"?

DAVON *dissolves. Weird hum ends.*

RACHAEL: *(Pouncing up on all fours.)* Jackson, You Dirty Rotten . . . *(Mouths words.)* Son-of-a-Bitch!

Audio: Over RACHAEL'S *last words: Good-Bad-Ugly's ey-ee-ey-ee-ah*

End Fifth Phase Video.

JACKSON: *(Appears in boat hole.)* Been a "long" day. 'Bout time fer some Beans.

Blackout.

Audio: Squeak begins.

SABBATH *enters* SL *and stands under red light* CS. *Red light rises on* SABBATH.

Scene: Campfire, moon and boat entry up (same).

Audio: Squeak ends.

JACKSON: Damn! Plumb forgot . . . 'at She'd "reappear"!

SABBATH: Dad?

JACKSON: No uh, Jackson.

SABBATH: Did you "find" Justine?

JACKSON: Weren't there.

SABBATH: I'm Way Sorry.

JACKSON: ul—She ain't, so Don't be.

SABBATH: Who?

JACKSON: *(Slowly exits boat crossing to fire.)* Whom. Your Daughter. What she asked on her "deathbed." *(Pause.)* She said, "Once that Damn Machine's a force, You Fix it So I'm never "born" . . .

(Slowly squatting next to fire.)

She Begged me 'til I swore but when the chance arose, I couldn't "then" . . . Though now despite My "mulish" aims, Justine won't ever die in pain.

Pause.

SABBATH: *(Crosses* SR—*stands behind* JACKSON.*)* Where's Yewell?

JACKSON: *(Looks up at* SABBATH.*)* uhhm-Not 'a this Earth.

SABBATH: And Racha-My "mother"?

JACKSON: *(Looks down at fire.)* She died givin' "birth."

Pause.

SABBATH: What happens to "Me"?

JACKSON: If you're set to go Home, I'll transport you Back.

SABBATH: But then You'll be Alone.

Pause.

JACKSON: Yeah well . . . *(Laughs.)* Won't lose any Sleep.

SABBATH: Hey! What If I "stay here" with You?

JACKSON: Countin' Sheep?

SABBATH: Huh?

JACKSON: Ain't much Exitement.

SABBATH: *(Looks around.)* It's Peaceful. *(Inhales.)* The Air's "clean" . . . *(Spinning around once.)* And I'm hella "Free"!

Pause.

SABBATH: *(Raises left hand.)* Um?

JACKSON: 'Kay?

SABBATH: Where's my Dad?

JACKSON: Wanna See?

SABBATH *nods.* JACKSON *enters boat.*

SABBATH: Like, Without the "past" . . . The Future wouldn't be.

Video begins.

SIXTH PHASE:
(Video)

Short to Woodstock; 1969.

DAVON *rides in back of an old pick-up after hitching a ride with* BUSTER *and* WOODCHUCK.

SHOT 1: DAVON FULL; BACK OF BUSTER AND WOODCHUCK'S (DRIVER) HEADS—FROM BED OF TRUCK

DAVON *eyes terrain* SL; BUSTER *and* WOODCHUCK *laugh engaged in unheard conversation.*

DAVON: *(Kneels smiling. Yells.)* Hey Man! This is Cool . . . *(Can't wait.)* Yeah!

WOODCHUCK *points;* BUSTER *pulls truck off to right and stops.*

DAVON: *(Jumping to ground.)* Jimi Fucking Hendrix!

SHOT 2: FROM WOODCHUCK'S OPEN WINDOW—DAVON OUTSIDE BUSTER'S OPEN WINDOW

DAVON: *(Bounces up to* BUSTER'S *open window.)* Like, Thanks . . . You Dude's 'r Righteous! *(Turns* SL.*)*

BUSTER *and* WOODCHUCK *look at each other—shrug;* DAVON *leaves frame.*

SHOT 3: DAVON—FULL SL TO TRUCK

DAVON: *(Looking up.)* This Time, I'm gonna Make "it"! *(Turning around.)*

SHOT 4: FROM BUSTER'S OPEN WINDOW

BUSTER: *(Turns head to* WOODCHUCK.*)* You know Sumpin' Woodchuck?

WOODCHUCK: *(Putting tranny into gear.)* What's That, Buster?

BUSTER: *(Looks ahead.)* These "kids" T'day Don't Give a Damn About the Future.

Truck pulls away with BUSTER *looking back.*

End of Sixth Phase video.

JACKSON: Woodstock, 1969.

SABBATH: Can we Bring my roommate Thalia Back?

JACKSON: *(Appears in boat—holds out hand for* SABBATH.*)* uh-Reckon.

Pause.

SABBATH *enters boat.*

All lights fade except campfire.

JACKSON: All in "time" . . .

Audio: Cricket chirps rise—boat entry light up low. On cue SABBATH *appears in boat hole lugging bucket.* SABBATH *goes to throw bucket of water on fire.*

Blackout.

Audio: Sound of water dowses fire. Cricket chirps slowly fade.

THE END